Fi
Cr
So
Something of

SOMETHING OF VALUE

DONNA FLETCHER CROW

VICTOR BOOKS®

A DIVISION OF SCRIPTURE PRESS PUBLICATIONS INC.
USA CANADA ENGLAND

Cover art by Ken Call, showing Mary Tudway and Rowland Hill
strolling along the Paragon in Bath. In the background,
the Countess of Huntingdon stands before her chapel.

Library of Congress Catalog Card Number: 87-62484
ISBN: 0-89693-354-7

VICTOR BOOKS
A division of SP Publications, Inc.
Wheaton, Illinois 60187

The Cambridge Collection

A Gentle Calling
(1749–1750)
John & Charles Wesley
George Whitefield
William Law
The Countess of Huntingdon

Something of Value
(1772–1773)
Charles Wesley
John Berridge
Rowland Hill
The Countess of Huntingdon

Brandley's Search
(1824)
Charles Simeon
Robert Hall

To Be Worthy
(1823–1825)
Charles Simeon
William Wilberforce

THERE ARE SO FEW PEOPLE now who want to have any intimate spiritual association with the eighteenth and nineteenth centuries . . .

Who bothers at all now about the work and achievement of our grandfathers, and how much of what they knew have we already forgotten?

DIETRICH BONHOEFFER, *Letters and Papers from Prison*

DONNA FLETCHER CROW brings a lifetime love of English literature and history as well as intensive research to The Cambridge Collection—her historical series on the work of the Evangelical Anglicans. A former English teacher, she is now a full-time writer. She and her husband, Stan, have four children.

THE TUDWAY & HILL FAMILIES

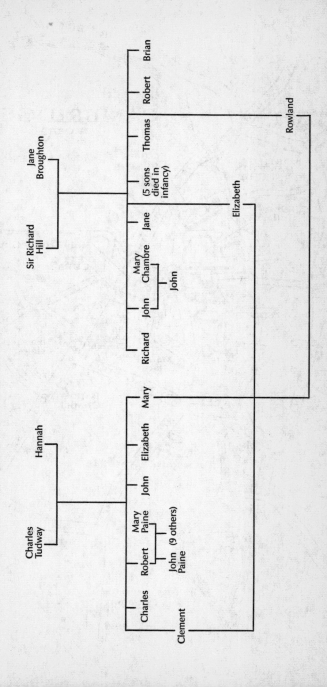

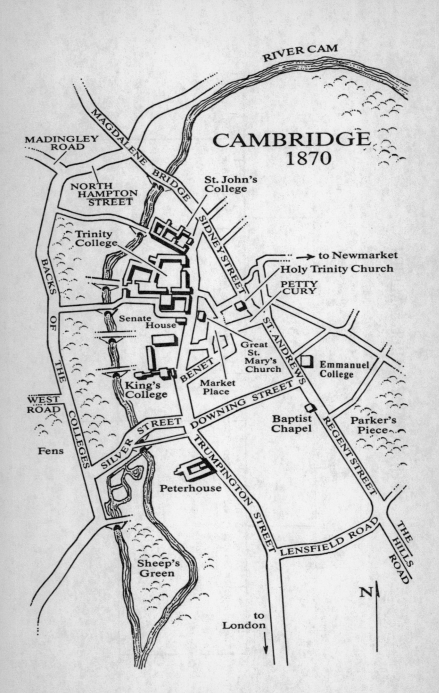

RIVER CAM

CAMBRIDGE
1870

MADINGLEY
ROAD

MAGDALENE BRIDGE

NORTH
HAMPTON
STREET

St. John's
College

SIDNEY STREET

Trinity
College

→ to Newmarket
Holy Trinity Church

PETTY
CURY

ST. ANDREWS

Senate
House

BACKS OF THE COLLEGES

BENET

Great
St.
Mary's
Church

Emmanuel
College

WEST
ROAD

King's
College

Market
Place

DOWNING STREET

Baptist
Chapel

Parker's
Piece

REGENT STREET

Fens

SILVER STREET

TRUMPINGTON STREET

Peterhouse

Sheep's
Green

LENSFIELD ROAD

THE HILLS ROAD

N

to
London

Miles 0 25 50 75

Kms 0 25 50 75

Newcastle

York

ENGLAND

Hawkstone
Sandon Hall

King's Cliffe

Cambridge

Troy House
Raglan
Bristol
Bath
Wells

Badminton

LONDON
Shoreham
Tunbridge Wells
Canterbury

Exeter

- - - - - the circuit ride

LONDON

St. John's Wood
Devonshire Place
Regent's Park
EUSTON ROAD
ALDERSGATE
The Foundry
MOORGATE
MARYLEBONE
Mary-lebone Church
Tottenham Court Chapel
CATO
EDGWARE ROAD
Lincoln's Inn
Piccadilly Circus
Paddington
OXFORD
PICCADILLY
St. James
FLEET
St. Paul's Cathedral
Bayswater
BAYSWATER ROAD
Hyde Park
Mayfair
PALL MALL
PARK
Kensington Gardens
Grosvenor Square
KNIGHTSBRIDGE
Ken-sington
KENSINGTON
South Kensington
Brompton
Buckingham Palace
London Bridge
to Osterley Park
OLD BROMPTON ROAD
Westminster Abbey
Surrey Lane Chapel
Chelsea
Parliament
Thames River
GROSVENOR ROAD

To Jennie Crow Speicher

*A gracious mother-in-law
is one of God's most precious gifts*

· 1 ·

"ROWLAND, YOU SIMPLY MUST give up this insane enthusiasm! You are accomplishing nothing but trouble for yourself and embarrassment for your family." Mary Tudway snapped shut her painted silk fan for emphasis. "Including the more distant members of your family." She stamped her foot to show how firmly she held her ground on this point.

"In other words, you find me an embarrassment." Rowland spoke slowly, almost in a drawl, his tall form relaxed and his brown eyes sparkling.

Mary's chin rose with her fury. She had no words adequate to express just how frustrating she found this man who managed to see humor even when she was fighting with him. But she was willing to use inadequate words. "You are an embarrassment and an irritant, and—and an infuriator, Sir!" She whirled and swept from the drawing room before she could soften under the gaze of his kind, humorous eyes.

But her triumphal exit was spoiled—she forgot that she was wearing her extra wide hoops, and she stuck in the doorway. Had Rowland laughed at her predicament, her temper would have forced her through the door even if it meant bending her hoops and tearing the chenille embroidery from her gown. But his soft entreaty, "Mary, please, let me speak," extinguished her anger as quickly as it had been ignited.

After his long fingers disengaged her hoop from the carved doorjamb where it had wedged, he held out his hand to lead her back into the room. She placed the tips of her fingers in the palm of his hand and followed him to the damask-covered sofa her mother had chosen to grace the south wall of the drawing room, when The Cedars was built fourteen years earlier.

Even though she had seemingly acquiesced to his plea that she let him speak, Mary was the first to begin. "Rowland, you know I regret my hasty temper. But I do not apologize for my sentiments. No one suggests you should give up your desire to take holy orders. That is most admirable and praiseworthy. With your distinguished family background, you will rise quickly and be able to hold a high office in the church. It is just this ridiculous Methodist notion you have taken into your head—"

"Mary—"

But she would not be silenced. "Your sister Elizabeth has spoken to me of it often. What if it were to be generally known in Wells, and the electorate refused to return my brother Clement to Parliament? Have you given no thought to the effect this enthusiasm you have espoused will have on those near you?"

"Mary—"

"Look at you! When we met at Clement and Elizabeth's wedding, I thought you the handsomest man I'd ever seen, in your red velvet coat embroidered in silver. And you danced the cotillion quite to perfection. Now you tell me you have given all that up for some religious maggot you've taken into your head."

"Mary—"

"Elizabeth says you are quite alone in your views at Cambridge and that the authorities are seriously alarmed by your activities. And she also says your mama is prostrate with worry. If you care nothing
for my opinion, you must care for hers."

"Mary—"

This time he was interrupted not by Mary, but by a bewigged and liveried footman anouncing that dinner was served in the dining room. Rowland bowed as Mary preceded him from the room, this time remembering to turn slightly sideways at the door. "Indeed, Mary, I thank you for granting me this interview. I do feel relieved at having been allowed to speak my mind." Again his eyes sparkled.

For all her outward poise, Mary went toward her family and guests feeling strangely shaken inside. It was nothing unusual for her to lose her temper, no matter how much she might wish it otherwise; nor was it unusual for her to speak the bold truth to any situation as she saw it, no matter how often her mama reminded her that tactful dissimulation would be more ladylike. But this confrontation with Rowland was different. Try as she might to tell herself that she was merely doing her duty to the family in attempting to urge her sister-in-law's brother to a more socially acceptable lifestyle, her innate honesty forced her to admit that her concern for Rowland Hill's affairs went beyond mere family duty.

She recalled their first meeting at Clement and Elizabeth's wedding. It had been one of the events of the season at the beautiful church of St. Marylebone in London, with an elaborate dinner following at the Hills' London home in Devonshire Place. She would never forget what generous notice Rowland took of her then. She was only a schoolroom miss, but her mama allowed her to dance three dances with family members. And she would never forget Rowland smiling at her so kindly, even when she tangled her feet in an intricate step and almost fell against him.

Since then, on occasions when the families were together for Christmas, Rowland would give her the most thoughtful gifts. She especially treasured her vellum-bound volume of Milton, even though she was now determined to read more fashionable poets.

Why had Rowland undertaken this course of action that could lead to nothing but disaster? She sighed. It seemed that even with all her arguments, there was nothing she could do to make him change. Of course, she knew he had espoused a personal faith for years—ever since his brother Richard was converted at Oxford and shared the experience with young Rowland at Eton. But visiting jails and hospitals was simply not done by people of consequence. Certainly not by a son of Richard Hill, Baronet, of Hawkstone, who could trace his family lineage back to Edward I and who was descended from Richard Hill, the first Protestant Lord Mayor of London and knighted by King Henry VIII.

The idea of one so descended being a Methodist was so impossible that it simply could not be. This was only a passing fancy of the sort undergraduates often took into their heads. Rowland would soon come to his senses.

She entered the anteroom and crossed to her mama who was chatting with their guests newly arrived from London. "Ah, here you are, Mary, my Dear. You have hidden yourself away from our guests and Sarah is simply bursting to talk to you, I'm sure."

17

Sarah Child flew to her with a flutter of silk skirts, lace flounces, and giggles. "Mary, I haven't seen you for such ages. I have the handsomest new beau to tell you about—"

Her disclosures were interrupted, however, as Mrs. Tudway led the guests into the dining room in strict order of rank, ladies first. A footman held the chair for her at the top of the table among all the women, with the most important female guests next to her. The master, Charles Tudway, sat among the men in order of rank at the bottom end of the table. For this dinner on the occasion of the visit of Mr. and Mrs. Robert Child of London and their daughter, Sarah, enroute to Bath, Hannah Tudway had strictly instructed the servants in the latest fashion of serving; rather than the guests helping themselves to dishes set on the table, the food was now served to them. The first course consisted mainly of meats—roasted, boiled, stewed, and fried, some with sauces. But the dish of which Charles Tudway was the proudest was served by the butler from a large silver soup tureen on the sideboard.

"Finest turtle soup you'll ever taste. My estate manager sends the turtles over regular from Antigua—always marked CT on the tail so there won't be any likelihood of my turtles being substituted for smaller ones bound for some house in London."

Robert Child took a rather noisy sip of his soup and decreed it to be much tastier and richer than any they had at Osterley Park.

"I'll have my manager send you a turtle," Tudway offered, in the spirit of convivial hospitality for which he was famous.

The men then fell to a general discussion of parliamentary events in London, kept lively with anecdotes from the two MPs seated at the table. Wells was represented in the House of Commons by Clement Tudway and his neighbor, Robert Child, a distant relative of the Robert Child of Osterley Park. Having two Robert Childs at the table added confusion as well as liveliness to the men's conversation.

At the ladies' end of the table, Hannah Tudway accepted one of the rich bread rolls known as whigs and turned to Mrs. Child on her right. "My dear Sarah, the fineness of your taste in decorating Osterley is quite famous. Perhaps you could just put a word in for me with Mr. Tudway. Don't you find this room somewhat lacking in ornamentation?"

Mrs. Child gazed around the elegant dining room with its rich paneling and ornate stuccoed ceiling. "The carved fireplace is one

18

of the finest I've ever seen. It rivals anything we have at Osterley–" She hesitated, looking at the marble-encased flames chasing the chill from the January night.

"Ah, you see my point precisely. The west wall is so plain, is it not? I have tried for months to persuade Mr. Tudway that we should have our portraits done by that fashionable Mr. Gainsborough who has set up his studio in Bath. Now, wouldn't that be just the thing to compliment the room?"

Mrs. Child agreed enthusiastically, and Mary smiled at the new strategy her mother's campaign was taking. Surely she was near to victory—the battle had been fought for so long. Squire Tudway had no desire to leave his lands and comfortable new home to go traipsing off to Bath to sit for "some fashionable dauber," but Hannah Tudway was determined and once her mind was made up, she could be quite insistent—a quality her daughter had inherited from her.

"This is famous," Mary said to Sarah who was seated next to her. "If Papa can be persuaded to go to Bath soon, we will be there while your mama is still taking the waters. I should like above all things to be in Bath with you."

Sarah returned her friend's smile. "We shall have ever so many beaux. Westmoreland has promised he will follow me to Bath. I can't fathom why Papa doesn't approve of him. He is prodigiously handsome, even if he does have a squint in one eye. But as soon as Papa returns to London and his musty old bank, Mama won't refuse to let me dance with anyone the Master of Ceremonies presents."

Mary was three years older than her friend; but Sarah, who had been raised in the social swirl of London society, was far more experienced in the ways of the world. The pampered only child of one of London's richest bankers, nothing had been denied Sarah Anne Child. Although Mary's embroidered cream satin gown was made by Wells' best dressmaker, she knew it lacked the French elegance of Sarah's brocaded white silk with undulating trails of flowers in shades of cream, green, and pink. And although Mary's brown hair was piled fashionably high on her head with one long curl caressing the side of her neck and a tiny lace cap perched on top, she knew that Sarah's hair, formed several inches higher than her own over a wire frame, far outdid hers in style. She thought of the fashionable beaux she and Sarah should spend their time danc-

19

ing with in Bath. Then she looked at Rowland, seated just down from her on the other side of the table. His head was thrown back in laughter at a mild witticism of her father's and the pose showed to perfection the excellent cut of his luxuriant brown hair, with the front brushed straight back and fairly high, and the back portion long, tied with a black ribbon which he brought round from the queue and tied in a bow over his fine lace cravat. Although she had berated him earlier for his lack of fashion, she had to admit he did look well in his cutaway coat and matching waistcoat of green poplin decorated with silk braid. If only he had instructed his tailor to add some gold embroidery and metallic lace. Ah, well, there would be plenty of handsome young men in fashionable coats to show her a good time in Bath.

Mary's papa, in his brown frock coat and bob-wig, was holding forth on his favorite subject to the men at his end of the table. "The latest letter from my manager in Antigua was full of distressing news. There has been a sudden fall in the price of sugars. But I am willing to hope the markets will certainly rise again—at present the market is overly full, that's all."

Both the Robert Childs and the two Tudway sons made agreeable comments and Squire Tudway continued. "I was also uneasy to hear that my rum on board *The McHeale* should have slipped the captain's memory. I am the more afraid it strengthened the memory of the sailors, for if the captain knew nothing of it being there, he certainly could have no care of it. I have known sailors to drink more than one-third of a vessel in a voyage and fill it up with water. But I hope this is not the case."

When the men went on to talk of the sheep on the Tudway estate at English Harbor, Antigua, Mary found her attention drawn again to the women's end of the table. Since her earliest memories of being allowed at the adult table, she had always enjoyed the conversation of her elders, and found their talk a doorway to another world. She early learned that if she sat very quietly, the adults conveniently forgot she was there and would discuss topics of business and politics which would not normally have been considered appropriate for the ears of a young girl.

But now the topic was most appropriate to Mary's interests; her sister-in-law Elizabeth had taken up the matter of sitting for a Gainsborough portrait. "Everyone of importance has a portrait done by him. I have made it clear to Clement that he simply must take time to do so, no matter how busy he may be in Parliament. If Father Tudway refuses to go to Bath, perhaps you could accompany Clement and me, Mother Tudway. I'm sure when he sees how handsome your portrait is, he'll agree to sitting for one of his own."

Mary smiled at this new advancement to her hopes and gave her attention to Sarah's chatter about the endless delights of the shops in Milsom Street. "All the finest shops in London have opened sister establishments in Bath—or some simply removed from London to Bath. They offer the greatest luxuries imaginable—"

Sarah went on to list the French silks, Belgian laces, and even items from the Orient available in Bath's endless variety of shops. On Mary's other side, the topic of business had been taken up by Sarah's father who was discussing the world of high finance in London's banking district. "But Child's Bank won't back such risky schemes as those. Yes, Sir, my family's been doing business for over a hundred years in No. 1 Fleet Street at the sign of the Marygold and I have no intention of weakening that position by backing a crackbrained scheme to settle New Zealand."

Francis, the Child ancestor who had established the family fortunes, had gone to London in 1642 to be apprenticed to a goldsmith. He married the daughter of another goldsmith and became established at the sign of the Marygold of which the present Child was so proud. The forward-looking Francis Child was among a number of London goldsmiths who went in for the profitable sideline of looking after other people's money. He eventually abandoned his original trade altogether and applied himself exclusively to banking. Although other goldsmiths quickly followed course, Child was the first to take the adventurous step, thereby earning for himself the title, The Father of Banking.

"Yes, Sir, there has been a Child doing business at the sign of the Marygold for one hundred ten years now, and if I have anything to say about it, there will be for another hundred and ten." Mary paused to wonder how this was to be accomplished, since Sarah was an only child and would take her husband's name even if she inherited the business. Well, perhaps there was a cousin bearing the Child name to carry on.

The circle of conversations had taken the diners through two courses, and now the servants entered bearing silver salvers with high pyramids of sweetmeats. The highest of the structures, a golden tower of candied apricots, was placed in the center of the table. Other three-sided pillars surrounded them in descending heights, offering the diners confections of dried fruits and nuts, tiny tarts filled with fairy butter or jams, and marchpan formed into tiny flowers and birds. She loved to take a variety of the designs on her plate and admire their cunning shapes and delicate colors. But she could never hold out for long against the sugared almond paste, and her plate was always clean of the confections before the meal was over. Almond sweetmeats were her greatest weakness; and in spite of Hannah Tudway's repeated warning to her daughter that she should grow quite stout if she continued to indulge, Mary's dressmaker assured her that her form was the most graceful she had the honor of dressing.

The servants departed and the diners returned to their conversations. The men had moved to their perennially favorite topic—politics, and Mr. Robert Child of Wells was recounting for his relative from London the contretemps of a recent election when there had been the first serious challenger for one of the seats held by Tudway and Child for more than ten years. The challenger, a Mr. Taylor, had been defeated, but the controversy still rankled, especially as *Pope's Bath Chronicle* had reported that the Mayor "did Mr. Taylor the favor to set down seven gentlemen as voting for him who in fact never appeared at the Assize Hall." In fact, it was found on a scrutiny that some fifty-five votes had been cast for their opponent by those who had no right of voting.

"Ah, but the outcome was a happy one, with the right men returned for the borough." The banker raised his glass of port. "The realm is in good hands with such sturdy men as yourselves in Parliament."

Mary noted throughout the meal the unusual quiet maintained by Rowland. He listened to the conversation with apparent interest and made appropriate comments along the way, but his usual liveliness seemed much suppressed. She hoped it wasn't the result of her earlier interview with him. She certainly wished for him to take her advice to heart, but she had no desire to wound him—although it was flattering to think he might care that much for her opinion.

Had her sharp words gone deeper than he showed at the time? Or were his problems with his family and the Cambridge authorities weighing on him more than he would admit? Ostracism couldn't be easy to bear, even for one so constantly cheerful as Rowland. Then a new thought struck her. How hard it must be for one of his temperament—who liked large, convivial groups, liked to be surrounded with friends and warm feelings, who should have been one of the most popular men at Cambridge—to be forced into virtual solitary confinement. Suddenly she had quite a different picture of Rowland than ever before, and her sympathetic nature, as quickly roused as her temper, reached out to him.

But Mary's reverie was brought to an end when the topic that had enthralled the ladies for the entire evening was picked up with renewed vigor at Elizabeth's comment, "Indeed, we must make our plans soon, before all the fashionable people are driven from Bath by the Countess of Huntingdon and her enthusiastic preachers."

Mary noted the long look this drew from Rowland, seated just down the table from Elizabeth, but he made no comment. To Mary's surprise, it was her mother who came to the Countess' defense. "It may well be that she goes too far, but I believe she did well in her fight to bring some moral fiber to the city against that libertine Beau Nash. I am told that it's not unusual for those who go to Bath to be cured of the gout often to find themselves with a new case of the disease—a sure sign of overindulgence in revels. I myself would not be averse to visiting the Countess' chapel while we're in Bath. I'm told Horace Walpole was most entertained there."

"Oh, no, not another church service," Sarah groaned. "One is obliged to attend the Abbey every day after breakfast. Surely that's quite enough care to be taken of one's soul."

For the first time that evening, the somewhat shy Maria, John Tudway's wife, put herself forward to make a speech. "But I should hope you won't attend the Countess during any regular services of the Abbey—that would show the greatest disrespect to the established church. My dear papa feels such behavior can lead to the gravest errors." Maria was the daughter of John Paine, a subdean of the Cathedral of Bath and Wells, and she was a loyal child of the established church. "Papa has warned me repeatedly against entanglements with enthusiasts."

Mary thought Rowland looked a little uncomfortable at this speech from the lady seated next to him. It gave Mary great satisfaction when she was able to catch his eye and give him a telling look.

Mrs. Child and Mrs. Tudway fell to discussing the advantages of the various baths the city offered, and a few moments later, Maria, who had been sitting between Rowland and Elizabeth, requested her mother-in-law's permission to leave the table. With a look that clearly expressed her hopes that Maria's desire for rest would soon be followed by an interesting announcement on the part of her second son and his wife, Mrs. Tudway nodded her approval. This left no one sitting between Elizabeth and her brother, so she turned to him directly and under the cover of the general conversation around the table said, "Rowly, I have had a letter from our mother. As I know you intend to depart early in the morning, I feel I simply must take this opportunity to speak to you most plainly."

As Elizabeth was obliged to talk across the empty space left by Maria, it was easier for Mary to follow their conversation—and far more interesting too—than the one to her left, where Mrs. Child was recounting with endless detail the instructions she had given her dressmaker for the ornamentation on Sarah's newest gowns.

"I am distressed to hear that my actions give pain to one so dear as my mother. Elizabeth, you know I would never choose to do so." The candlelight shone on his long face with the square jaw, heavy eyebrows, and kind mouth.

"Then, Rowland, you must give up this course you are pursuing. Enthusiasm can only bring disgrace upon yourself and the entire family. Papa has received a letter from the Master of St. John's." Elizabeth paused for emphasis.

"Yes?" The tight voice with which the single word was spoken revealed Rowland's nervousness.

"If you continue to visit the prisons and hospitals and preach in the fields around Cambridge, you will force the authorities to take action. Rowland, you must give this up."

"But no one tells Richard he must give up his faith. No one tells Jane she has disgraced the family by espousing a personal religion."

"Your personal faith is a private matter and I do not speak of it. It is your activities. Why cannot you behave as other young men your age? All of England, except a few Jews, are Christian—why must you make public display of it?"

"To him that knoweth to do good and doeth it not, it is sin." Rowland spoke quietly. Mary could see that this was one situation he did not find humorous.

24

"But does not the fact that you are the only one who believes so in your entire class of thirty-two gownsmen indicate to you that perhaps it is you who are wrong?"

"Nay, Sister, it is you who are wrong." And Mary noted that the sparkle had come back into his eyes. "In the entire University there are three others who would be identified as Christians."

"My point precisely. A total of four gownsmen and no master or dons?"

"I fear not. But the shoeblack at the gate always has a smile for me. Indeed, for the first year I was there, until I found my three friends, he was the only one in the Universtiy who would smile at me. But truly, our numbers have grown."

With her recent understanding of the real situation, Mary knew that the humor he evidenced was self-deprecating and not his true view of the unfortunate circumstance.

Later that evening when the final guests were departing and Rowland took his leave of Mary, he again showed no sign of humor as he said, "Mary, I am to return to Cambridge for my final term. If all goes well, I should be ordained by summer. When that is accomplished, I wish to speak to you more to the point."

His words elated Mary and confused her so that it was impossible for her to form a reply.

But fortunately, his rapid departure made speech on her part unnecessary and left her standing in the hall with the warm memory of his lips just brushing her fingertips as lightly as if she had dreamed it. His words left no doubt of their meaning; yet what could he be thinking? Did he expect her to marry a Methodist? Then she smiled with a brilliance born of new hope. If he truly cared for her as deeply as his words indicated, he surely would change his actions. On their next meeting she would persuade him. It was only a matter of time until Rowland Hill would be a sensible young man.

· 2 ·

IT WAS TO BE SOME TIME, however, before Mary had her chance at persuasion. A few weeks later, Rowland sat with a newly enlarged group of gownsmen in his rooms at St. John's, Cambridge, studying together the Greek New Testament, as had become their habit every evening after Hall. " 'But as many as received Him, to them gave He power to become the sons of God—' "

"Sorry to interrupt, Penty." Rowland looked up from his open Bible to the serious faces before him. "But I believe the word you construed as 'power' is better translated 'right.' It doesn't describe mere ability, but legitimate, rightful authority, derived from a competent source, which includes but goes beyond the idea of power."

Pentycross, the gownsman who had been reading, nodded, and their friend Simpson added, "Yes, that's an important distinction; in the Incarnation God made adequate provision for men to have the right, based on proper authority and power, to become the children of God."

"I daresay you're right about that," said Robinson, a short, blond fellow seated next to Rowland. "But my brain has had all the Greek it cares for tonight, and I still need to read that passage of Locke before lecture tomorrow."

Frampton, a newcomer to the circle, looked at Rowland and the three others who had spoken and shook his head. "I'm afraid my brain has had quite a bit more than it cares for. Did you say you fellows have been swatting away at this for years—on your own?"

Rowland smiled at the twelve men in his room. "Ah, now we are

26

a veritable houseful—twelve of us just like the early disciples. But for my first years here, Penty, Sim, Robinson, and I had to make do with one another's company en toto."

"Which wouldn't have been so bad," Pentycross grinned, "except that it meant putting up with Hill's little jokes."

"An unhealthy situation, you'll agree." Simpson waved at the air around him as if to clear away the harmful humors.

"Ah, yes," Rowland nodded. "I have always been most grateful to the letter H, for without it I should have been ill all my life."

The gownsmen's groans were interrupted by Rowland's somber gyp Bottisham bringing in a tray of coffee. But a short time later, over steaming cups of the milky liquid, the conversation turned serious again as the freshman Frampton said, "But it does seem to me that since St. John's is a richly gifted college in livings, and so many of the gownsmen look forward to a clerical life, the college preparation which consists solely in a chapter or so of weekly Greek construing from the Gospels is hardly adequate."

"Which is why we read together on our own, no matter how frowned upon such activity is by the authorities," Robinson said. "Of course, we are also required to be present at a certain number of divinity lectures in the schools—but not one word do we ever hear of the early church, of the fathers of the faith, or of the doctrines of Christianity. We have Locke and Aristophanes, but not one work of true religion."

For the first time Simpson displayed his quick temper. "And so the young gentlemen obtain college prizes, proceed to ordination, and have livings bestowed upon them. After which they grow large, read the *Quarterly Review*, and die at last of fat rot. These, my friends, are the clerical gentlemen of England."

Frampton set his cup down and drew back in his chair. "Surely you are a bit harsh."

Rowland replied, "The clergy are not entirely to blame. They are given no instruction in Christian doctrine. Every word of the mysteries of faith is as strange to their minds as if they were Mohammedans or Chinese bonzes. Some of the serious clergy have, in full manhood, been converted from a life of previous debauchery to a sense of their sinful lives, and so brought to deep repentance. They then for the first time begin to read the Scriptures, and are thus launched into the mighty ocean of true knowledge of God."

27

But Rowland's words had little calming effect upon Simpson. "The University of Cambridge produces half the religion of the kingdom. It is an ever-teeming fountain of bishops, priests, and deacons. The Masters of colleges are mostly dignitaries of the church, and two-thirds of all the fellows of the colleges are priests. And yet, religion at Cambridge is entirely theatrical; everything is done for show. All is pomp and ceremonies—white linen and scarlet robes, wax candles, organs, anthems, and processions."

"But not just at Cambidge," Robinson said in a hearty manner that indicated his listeners should somehow find his words encouraging. "The general style of preaching throughout England is dry, profitless, dull, and antichristian. The Gospel is quite unknown, and indeed is scarcely ever alluded to. They preach about virtue and justification by good works, a little against enthusiasm, and a good deal about the duty of being an Englishman."

"And when our small number is gone, who shall be here to light the flame in all this darkness?" Pentycross asked.

Rowland Hill nodded. "I too have given that serious consideration. I am convinced that we must pray heartily for the next generation of Cambridge students, that they will have someone to lead them in the way."

"As you have led us, Hill," Frampton said.

Rowland shook his head. "I have done nothing. What is needed is someone in authority, a Fellow or Master who can teach openly. Who knows, the Lord may be preparing even now to raise someone up. I was back at Eton to visit my old Master only a week ago and met a young school boy who exhibited a most unusually serious turn of mind. Simeon was his name, Charles Simeon."

After his companions departed, Rowland paused for his own prayers before going to bed. At first he interceded for his fellow gownsmen, then for those he preached to around Cambridge, and finally for his own family. But he found his mind repeatedly straying to thoughts of Mary. His last interview with her had been far from satisfactory, and her heated words that he should give up irregular preaching stung his memory. He had cared deeply for her for many years, but he would not give up his preaching even for her. "I love God more than her," he thought, as he snuffed out his candle. But the thought was not a cheering one.

The next morning, Rowland found nothing to comfort him but

his naturally buoyant nature and his faith in God's lordship over all. The morning's lecture on Locke was cold and sterile, but less numbing than the compulsory chapel service that followed it. Rowland couldn't help wondering if required chapel attendance wasn't a positive evil. At that moment he could conceive of nothing worse than forcing undergraduates to attend chapel and take the sacraments. The Scripture was clear that one should not partake unworthily, and yet the system forced troops of young profligates to receive the Lord's Supper.

" '. . . Therefore with angels and archangels, and with all the company of heaven, we laud and magnify Thy glorious Name, evermore praising Thee, and saying, Holy, holy holy, Lord God of hosts, heaven and earth are full of Thy glory; Glory be to Thee, O Lord most High. Amen.' " The priest monotoned at such nonstop speed that, had Rowland not known the words by heart, he would have had no idea what was being said.

Their black academical robes and caps whipped by the spring wind that whistled through First Court, Rowland and Pentycross left the chapel, crossed into Second Court under the statue of the college foundress, Lady Margaret Beaufort, and went up the staircase to Rowland's rooms.

Crossing the larger outer room where the group had met the night before, they went on to the inner sanctum, as Rowland called it. This was a smaller, cozier room, with a well-worn green carpet and a case of his most cherished books. Pentycross was bent on continuing the topic of the night before, with an anecdote of the time he went out shooting with a local clergyman. "We were some two or three miles from Cambridge when he said to me, 'We must go on a little to the right to St. Mark's church. I have promised to take a funeral there at three o'clock.' We reached it in time and stopped at the outer gate. 'Keep the dog and my gun,' quoth he. He leaned the gun by the gate, tucked up his trousers into breeches, went in, performed the funeral, came forth, took up his gun, patted doggie on the head, and we went on as before shooting our way home. Now I ask you, Hill, would you like to be buried by such a priest?"

"Indeed, not." Rowland rang the bell for his gyp to bring their morning coffee. "I should not like to be buried by any priest just at the moment. There are a number of things I hope to accomplish before I have the honor to choose a priest for my funeral sermon."

"Fah, Hill!"

Rowland held up his hand, "No, no. I quite take your point; it is distressing that so little comfort should be given or so little good accomplished at such a time."

The stoop-shouldered, long-faced Bottisham entered, as always, as if the bell he answered knelled his eternal doom. "Nice to see you looking your usual cheerful self this morning, Bottisham." Rowland took his coffee and the morning post the college servant held out to him. "Ah, riches indeed. Three letters in the post." He started to set them aside, then noted that the top one was from John Berridge, rector of the nearby village of Everton, who served as mentor to the young band of Cambridge Christians. "This one's from Berridge. Shall I read it out?" As Pentycross agreed, he began.

"Dear Rowly,

My heart sends you some of its kindest love, and breathes its tenderest wishes for you. How soft and sweet are those silken cords which the dear Redeemer twines and ties about the hearts of His children!

I hope you will have leisure to call upon me soon at Everton. Until then may grace, mercy, and peace be with you. May heavenly truth beam into your soul, and heavenly love inflame your heart.

Be faithful and diligent, and look up to your Master continually for direction and assistance. Remember His gracious promise, "Lo, I am with you alway, even unto the end of the world." He will supply you with wisdom, strength, and courage, for He sends none upon a warfare at their own cost.

Go out, therefore, and work whilst the day lasteth; and may the Lord Jesus water your own soul, and give ten thousand seals to your ministry. I am with great affection your

J. Berridge"

Rowland looked puzzled. "I wonder what prompted that?"

Pentycross shrugged. "He has undoubtedly heard of the official objections over your preaching to those in prison and visiting the sick and motherless."

"Yes, I suppose that's all. Well, I must call on him soon."

Rowland smiled and sipped his coffee, but he was unusually quiet and a small frown creased his forehead.

"Do you preach at the Castle today?" Pentycross asked, as he set down his empty cup.

"Yes. In about an hour's time. Will you go with me?"

Pentycross nodded, agreed to meet him at the Magdalen Bridge, and then took his leave.

Rowland turned to his unopened post and broke the red seal on a missive in his father's unmistakable, powerful handwriting. He had read only a few lines when he knew he was glad he had read Berridge's words of encouragement first, because his father's were far from encouraging.

. . . and, therefore, I hope to hear you have renounced this irregular preaching. Your mother and I deeply regret this signal mark of indifference to the establishment, which we fear might soon strengthen into defiance of its power and renunciation of its principles.

Your activities are such as to represent you as a headstrong and heedless zealot. Such a hopeless branch many would cut off and leave to take root and flourish where he could, or wither through want of stability and support. It is through the influence and intercession of your brother Richard, however, that I will not take such a drastic step. You must know, though, that, if such activities continue on your part, I will be forced to reduce your allowance, at the very least.

The homily continued to the bottom of the page and Rowland read it dutifully, then put it down sadly. He would never willingly do anything to hurt or embarrass his family. He was proud of his pedigree, and hoped his family could be proud of him. But his allegiance to his Heavenly Father demanded first place.

He turned with relief to the third letter, this also from his family seat, Hawkstone, but in his brother Richard's hand. Here he would find support and encouragement from one who understood his heart and shared his faith.

Yet even this letter failed to provide its looked-for consolation. Richard wrote to inform him of storm clouds gathering at Oxford over the heads of a small band of Christians very like his own society at Cambridge. Because of their unity of sentiments, Rowland had kept up a lively correspondence with his counterparts at Oxford and had encouraged them in their religious exercise. But it was several weeks since he had heard from his friends there, and now he learned why. For some time the Oxford group had been meeting in the house of a widow who was a friend of George Whitefield. But their activities had come to the attention of the college authorites.

. . . In spite of repeated warnings from the dons, our friends think it cowardly to desist, even though they are threatened with loss of character, degrees, orders, and even expulsion itself.

Our friend Mr. Hallward assures me that they are unmoved by these things, and that for his part he "considers it a happiness and privilege to be counted worthy to suffer reproach for Jesus' sake with the little flock."

Dear Rowly, you must proceed cautiously that you not bring similar recriminations upon your own head. In Oxford the lion has roared, though I think he has had but little real cause. Beware you give him not cause in Cambridge.

I am your ever faithful bro,

Richard

Rowland dropped the letter on the table. How much more must he bear? First Mary, then Elizabeth, then their father, and now, *Richard*, who had always been his strongest encourager, who most truly understood his urgency to preach. That Richard should ask him to pull back in his efforts—

He wasn't even aware of the knock on his door until Pearce, his tutor, stood before him. "Hill, I have come from the Master with the gravest news. He is determined to expel you unless you cease conventicling."

Rowland looked at his tall, broad-shouldered tutor, his dark hair tied back in a neat queue. "My irregular meetings may not be sanctioned by man, but they are sanctioned by a Higher Power. Which would you have me obey, Pearce?"

Suddenly he smiled. It was as if this blow, coming after what he had thought to be the final stroke, instead of making him crumple, fueled his determination. "Do not look so dismal, Pearce. I know you are on my side and want only the best. And I know how it is with the authorities. Much good has been done lately in the town and in the University, so they naturally suppose me to be at the bottom of it. Well, I may be at the bottom of it, but I'm not at the top—the Lord is King."

But Pearce was not mollified. "Hill, it is because I am as much your friend as ever that I am exceedingly anxious for you to continue in college. At first I thought the Master agreed to my plea. But then he seemed sorry for what he had granted. He does not accuse you of any fresh disobedience. It is yet again the old score—if you are to stay in college, he insists upon your promising never to make any more converts in the University or to go into any house in the town to offer relief. And you must give all your alms into the hands of others to dispense for you."

Rowland rose to his full height and took several quick strides around the room on his long legs. At last he came to a stop directly in front of his tutor and spoke as forcefully as if he had been addressing the Master of St. John's himself. "These terms are utterly against my conscience. I never could consent to them. My activities are by no means against any law of God or of man. I would sooner leave the University than stay upon such terms."

There was absolute silence in the room as Pearce took full account of his words. Then with a small nod of his head, he said, "I will go again to the Master." He gave Rowland a firm handclasp before he left the room.

"Well, at least he didn't forbid preaching in the prison," Rowland said to the closed door, then shrugged into his wool coat and tugged the inch-wide frills of his linen shirt out from the narrow coat sleeves. He picked up his tricorn hat, walking stick, and well-worn Bible and prayer book, then closed the door firmly behind him, as if shutting all controversy and opposition into the room and leaving him free to proceed.

The afternoon was as blustery as the morning had been, and Rowland shivered as he crossed First Court, went past the ancient chapel and out the main gate. He paused beneath the statue of St. John bearing the arms of the college foundress and a bunch of marguerites for her name, Lady Margaret. Before 1500 the site had been occupied by a hospital run by a religious community; when the community dwindled, Lady Margaret chose the location on the banks of the River Cam for her college, which became a center of

Renaissance scholarship. Rowland took a vague comfort from the fact that for centuries the ground had been hallowed by service to needy men and to the glory of God.

"Good day," Rowland greeted his faithful friend the shoeblack, at his place of business just outside the gate.

The man's weathered, wrinkled face broke into a smile made brilliant by his white teeth and round eyes. "Good day, Mr. Hill. The good Lord bless you. You want me to black your shoes today? Free for you, as always."

"Thank you, Cobbleton. I appreciate the offer, but they'll need it a lot worse when I come back down the hill."

"You goin' to preach to the captive souls, eh?" He smiled at his own joke. "Well, God give you freedom."

Another gownsman approached with shoes clearly in need of Cobbleton's services and Rowland waved his farewell as he turned toward the river. At the bridge he met Pentycross, and the two continued up the slight incline of Magdalen Street that had once been Castle Hill. Only a mound remained to mark what had been Cambridge Castle in medieval times. The Castle had been little used since the fifteenth century and had fallen into ruins. All that now remained was the gatehouse which was used as a prison.

Rowland was a familiar figure to warders and prisoners alike and had no trouble gaining admission. After all the opposition he had faced recently, the prison seemed almost friendly; but he was still grateful for the companionship of Pentycross. The turnkey showed them into the largest of the common cells. Unlike the rowdy, egg-throwing townies and sneering, supercilious gownsmen he encountered when he preached in the marketplace, Rowland's congregation at the Castle prison was grateful for any break in the boredom of their lives. Whether they listened for spiritual counsel or merely for entertainment, at least they listened.

"Ah, tis Parson 'ill, climbed the 'ill to bring us a word, 'ave ye?" The words whistled through the spaces in the old man's teeth.

"That's right, Nettle. Didn't think I'd forget you, did you?"

"Ye might as well. All else of 'um 'ast."

"No, my friend, not quite all. The Lord hasn't forgotten you."

"Nor 'as ta grim reaper. Old Jones died o' the grippe three days past. Death an' disease don't forget no one."

Rowland looked around the filthy cell to include everyone in his reply to Nettle. "May God bring you to the only remedy against

34

that most direful of diseases—sin. This poor sinner who speaks to you found the remedy at the foot of the Cross.

"In this dark place we need to let the light shine—the light of God's love. We cannot shine with rays of our own, but we can shine if shown upon."

As Rowland spoke, a deep quiet descended on the rough, untutored worshipers, as if the old stones of the Castle gatehouse were hallowed ground. The sense of reverence touched Rowland's own rapidly beating heart as he looked from face to face; a few stood out clearly—the grizzled Nettle who always greeted him with the latest news of their small community, imprisoned for debts that probably would never be paid; the sneering but attentive Jakeman, proud of his escapades as a thief and likely to return to them unless God changed his heart; Gastard, the youngest of the prisoners—

At the end of the service Rowland prayed extempore, the light in the cell being too dim to read from the prayer book. Then he and Penty retraced their steps back down Castle Hill. Pentycross chatted about the service and college affairs, but Rowland hardly attended, simply nodding at intervals when his friend paused.

"You all right, Hill?" Penty asked, when they reached St. John's gate. "Never knew you to keep quiet so long altogether."

Rowland smiled at his friend. "Yes, I believe I'm very much all right. Thank you for accompanying me. Must hurry now; not good form to be late for Hall."

Back in his rooms, putting on the satin knee breaches and heavily embroidered coat required for college dining, Rowland was able to define the feeling that had been growing on him since the service at the Castle. It was the most wonderful sense of release. Whatever the outcome with the college authorities, he had done right.

"Some hot water, please, Bottisham." He sent his gyp out of the room so he could exult in the experience alone. When the door closed, he flung out his arms to embrace all of God's world and threw his head back and laughed—a deep, rich laughter that came from his heart and winged upward to heaven like a prayer.

He might have continued laughing until Bottisham returned had he not caught sight of the hastily discarded letters on his table and been reminded again of his family's disapproval. Rowland could be sure in his own mind and heart that he was doing right, but how would he convince those dearest to him?

35

· 3 ·

NOTHING WAS further from Mary's mind than preaching in a prison. At high noon, the Tudway coach-and-four rolled past the fashionable shops that lined the Pulteney Bridge spanning the Avon River, and made a triumphal entry into the city Mrs. Tudway had campaigned so stalwartly to visit. Squire Tudway had not submitted to the trip to Bath himself, but made no objection to his wife and daughter accompanying Elizabeth and Clement. And so, after days of flurried packing and last-minute calls to the dressmaker, Mary was making her first visit to the fashionable spa.

Bath, city of graceful spires and ringing bells, of golden buildings each as beautiful as an artist's sculpture, city of glorious parks and flowers against a hillside of emerald greenness, of the greatest elegance the aristocracy of England could produce, welcomed Mary Tudway. The bells, decreed by Beau Nash to ring welcome to important new arrivals, pealed and echoed against the blue March sky, and Mary knew she had never been happier. This gaity was what she had longed for, cloistered as she had been in the quiet cathedral city of Wells. Beaux and courtesans, macaronies and the cream of society—here all met and held revel, and she, Mary Tudway, would enter into their marvelously brilliant company.

As the coach turned into Broad Street, Mary's head felt like a shuttlecock as she turned from side to side, trying to take in the shops and the teeming parade of fashion. Ladies of great elegance, with coiffures almost a foot high, swept up the street followed by maids and pages carrying colorful bandboxes; ornate gilt and tapes-

36

try sedan chairs bearing ladies of even greater dignity than those on the walks were borne on poles by liveried chairmen. And then, Mary, who thought she was prepared for any sight her senses could present, cried in astonishment, "Oh, pray tell, Elizabeth—are those macaronies?"

Elizabeth bent her head carefully so as not to hit her headdress on the panels of the coach and looked in the direction Mary was pointing. "Indeed they are," she laughed. "But perhaps rather restrained ones."

The two young swells walked slowly so all might have the advantage of viewing their startling beauty. The one closer to the Tudway carriage wore a white wig which towered high; on top of it perched a tiny tricorn hat. At that moment a lady of his acquaintance approached, requiring him to employ his gold-knobbed, tasseled cane to raise his hat to her, since the hat was well beyond the reach of his arm.

His companion, clad in a form-fitting suit in startling shades of scarlet and cerise, flicked open a jeweled snuffbox before making the lady an elegant leg, and then tottered on up the street on his three-inch-high red heels.

Mary was now turned around in her seat watching the amazing sight through the rear window. "Restrained?" she gasped.

Elizabeth smiled. "Well, not *too* restrained. But since the supreme goal in life to all members of the Macaroni Club is to be different, you may meet some more alarming specimens yet."

"Elizabeth," Mrs. Tudway spoke sharply, "I hope you use the term 'meet' loosely. My daughter may *see* such oddities, but I do not want any such ridiculous fops presented to her."

Elizabeth was immediately as serious as her mother-in-law. "Certainly, Mother Tudway. That would be most unsuitable. I shall watch carefully that none but the most proper young men are introduced to Mary."

Mary gritted her teeth. What was the good of coming to a fashionable spa if one could meet only suitable people? There were plenty such people in Wells—canons, deacons, worthy squires like her father and brothers. As she drank in the heady atmosphere around her, she realized more sharply than ever just how circumscribed her life had been. Since her come-out two years before, she had attended all the city offered—fetes at the Bishop's Palace, picnics in the summer, dinner parties with the local gentry. It had

37

been just enough to whet her appetite for more fun and fashion. And before that there had been yearly trips to London, with extended stays when Papa was in Parliament; but she had been a schoolroom miss then, never out from under the careful eye of her governess, Miss Fossbenner. And Mary had quickly learned that pianoforte, embroidery, French, and watercolor lessons were quite as dull in London as in Wells, even when relieved by a carefully supervised outing to a museum or park. There was certainly never a glimpse of such amusements as the elegant Vauxhall Gardens she had read and dreamed of, with its grand promenades, fireworks displays, and even masquerade parties.

Mary's active imagination had fed richly on such scenes, and letters from her father's estate manager in Antigua telling of life in that faraway island with strange people and exotic customs fired her daydreams. Well, she wasn't in Antigua or in London, but Bath would do very well for the moment. She hadn't even brought any of her needlework with her. And now that she was out, the next time she could persuade her papa to take her to London—who knew what delights would be waiting for her?

The coach swept around the Circus, a magnificent circle of homes designed in the classical style by John Wood the Elder, with a green park in the center. "O Clement, how grand. I wish we could have taken rooms here," Mary cried.

"Just wait, little Sister, I have done better for you. The Circus is very fashionable, but offers no view except of one's neighbor. I find the Royal Crescent much more to my liking."

The coach rattled to the end of Brook Street and Mary gasped at the sight of a vast green lawn sweeping up the steep hillside to a crescent of buildings even more beautiful than the Circus. "It is considered to be the finest crescent in Europe," Clement said. "I would not dispute that, but it is the view, offering a vista clear down to the Avon, that made it my choice. Also the fact that the Childs are staying here. I thought our mother would be most comfortable with neighbors she already knows."

Mrs. Tudway beamed her approval. "Excellent, Clement, very well done."

When the coach stopped before Number Six, Clement ushered the ladies into the entrance hall, hung with paper skillfully marbled to resemble a golden, Italian terrazo, then held open the door of the drawing room with its green silk damask wallhangings, melon-colored Chippendale sofa, and amber Axminster carpet. "I'll tell Benson to send in a dish of bohea while the luggage is being attended to." Clement turned to direct the servants he had sent ahead from their home in Wells.

But Mary could not sit still and drink tea. She wandered around the room, admiring the marble fireplace, the pianoforte, the chandelier of Bristol glass, wondering how long she could contain her impatience to explore more of the city. She wasn't required to wait long, though, for Benson quickly returned to announce Mrs. Child and Miss Child.

"My dear Sarah!" This time it was Mary who flew to her friend. "We have come! Isn't it famous! Just as we planned!"

The girls sat on small velvet chairs, their heads bent together as Sarah chattered on. "Everyone rises at six for a soak at the hot baths. The doctor says Mama must bathe every day and I often accompany her. Then we assemble in the Pump Room. The water is unspeakably foul, but you won't be obliged to drink it. Mr. King, the Master of Ceremonies—everyone says he's quite as good at it as that autocratic Beau Nash who set all his fusty rules—every morning picks out the finest beau in the room to present to me. Mama is very careful that he not introduce any gazetted fortunehunters; but after all, that is why one relies on a Master of Ceremonies, to keep off the undesirables. There must be enough of them in a place like this."

Mary interrupted to describe the macaronies she had seen. Then Sarah continued, detailing the schedule Mary should begin the following day. "After the Pump Room everyone takes breakfast. Now that the weather is warmer, perhaps we may get up a party to Spring Gardens across the river. Then there's holy service at the Abbey. Really, one must go—it's quite *de rigeur* to be seen there— and of course, only the quality attend, so one can always hope to meet a beau to escort one to the bookstore or the shops afterward."

Sarah might have gone on longer, as she was only to midafternoon in recounting her daily routine, but Mrs. Child had completed her errand to invite the new arrivals to dinner late that afternoon. Mrs. Tudway declined, saying she should prefer to eat in her own dining room on her first night in town. And much to Mary's agitation, she also declined the invitation to attend the Assembly Room ball that evening, on the grounds that after their journey they should all have an early night. It would be quite soon enough to begin in the morning.

So it was with anticipation simmering almost to the boiling point that Mary entered the Pump Room the next morning. "If you will stay here just a moment, I will attempt to secure a table," Clement said to his mother. And Mary was indeed happy just to stand and survey the great room. Around the walls, Corinthian columns rose white and gold. At the far end of the room in a galleried alcove, a trio of musicians played a lively Haydn air for those promenading around the room in elegant dishabille, after their morning baths. Along the wall to her left was a smaller alcove, backed by tall French doors; and as the company filling the room gave opportunity, Mary could see the pumpers at work behind a counter, serving glasses of Bath's famous mineral water. And indeed, the invalids leaning on sticks, or being pushed around the room in wicker Bath chairs, their heavily bandaged, gouty feet elevated for comfort, told of the popularity of the remedy.

"We are in luck," Clement announced upon his return. "There are no tables available, but Mrs. Child has invited us to join her party." Clement led the way to the center of the room where mahogany Sheraton chairs clustered around small tables.

Clement then departed to obtain the mineral water—everyone was expected to down three glasses of the health-giving liquid. Even before he returned, the Master of Ceremonies was begging Mrs. Child to present the new members of her company. Mr. King wore a cream-colored, three-cornered hat and gold-frogged, lace-edged coat over an embroidered waistcoat and ruffled shirt—as complete a replica as possible of the deceased Beau Nash whose shoes he attempted to fill. When the introductions were completed, he chatted for a few moments with Mrs. Tudway and Elizabeth, welcoming them to Bath, then bowed his leave-taking. But in a very few minutes he returned with two young gentlemen in tow.

Mary's heart leapt at the sight of the shorter and more handsome of the two. His powdered hair was arranged with just the right amount of curl and elevation to accent his classic aquiline nose and fine cheekbones, just as the particular shade of blue-green ribbed silk from which his coat and breeches were cut emphasized the color of his eyes; the exquisite chenille embroidery and silver sequin ornamentation of his waistcoat told he was a gentleman of the finest taste.

40

"Miss Tudway, may I have the great honor of presenting Roger Twysden, nephew of the Bishop of Raphoe," Mr. King said. The nephew of a bishop. Even her careful father couldn't fault such a family. Mary smiled radiantly as Mr. Twysden bowed over her hand.

A sharp jab in her ribs from Sarah brought Mary back to attention and she realized the Master of Ceremonies had completed his duties and departed, leaving them each with a beau, just as Sarah had foretold. But the suppressed excitement on Sarah's face told her something special was afoot.

"Mary, you were quite lost when Mr. King made his introductions. Now I must do it all over again. May I present John Fane, the Earl of Westmoreland. You will hear his friends call him Rapid, I believe."

Mary acknowledged the introduction as it had been given, as if this were the first meeting between Sarah and His Lordship; but she was certain this was the beau Sarah had told her of in excited whispers at The Cedars—the one her father disapproved of, but who had sworn to follow her to Bath. Mrs. Child, deep in gossip with Elizabeth and Hannah Tudway, showed no disapproval, however; and as Mr. Child was in faraway London toiling at his sign of the Marygold, there seemed to be no threat to Sarah's happiness.

And a short time later, when Mrs. Child accepted Westmoreland's invitation for the company to join him at a concert breakfast at the Assembly Room for which he held tickets, Mary's suspicion was confirmed—either Mrs. Child didn't know of or didn't share her husband's disapproval.

At that moment, there was a stir in the crowd as a small, severe-looking woman in a dark green gown, and full white headdress that gave the effect of a prioress, entered through the French doors that opened onto the courtyard. An assortment of followers trailed behind at a respectful distance, but Mary's attention was caught by the sweet-looking young woman, older than herself by perhaps six years, in a gown of heavy ivory satin over a pale blue petticoat.

"Egad," Roger said with a flip of the lace handkerchief he carried. "It's Her Holiness, the Countess of Huntingdon, honoring us with her presence. Probably come to lead in prayers or bless the water or something."

The Master of Ceremonies rushed forward to greet Her Ladyship and escort her party to a hastily prepared table near the musi-

41

cians' gallery. Mr. King himself brought glasses of water to the Countess' table.

Mary turned to gain a clearer view of the celebrated lady. "And who is the young woman with her—the pretty one?"

Sarah leaned closer and answered Mary's question. "That's Lady Selina, the Countess' daughter. She's really perfectly amiable, for all she embraces her mama's fusty theology."

"I hope I shall have opportunity to meet her."

The words were no more than out of Mary's mouth than Elizabeth spoke up. "I believe I should pay my respects to Her Ladyship. The Countess is a great encourager of my brother; and before his death, her chaplain, Mr. Whitefield, wrote Rowland numerous letters boosting his faith."

For a moment Mary was stunned. In the excitement of Bath she had all but forgotten the young man who so recently had caused her such emotional stir. This great lady had taken notice of him? And he had come under the tutelage of the famous George Whitefield? She had no idea that Rowland had caught the attention of such noted personages. What could he have done to merit such marks of condescension?

But Mary's questions went unanswered as, at Elizabeth's bidding, Clement hurried off to secure Mr. King's services to present their party to the Countess.

"Ah yes. The sister of our dear Rowly," Lady Huntingdon said to Elizabeth a few minutes later, casting a sharp eye at Elizabeth's fashionably low-cut neckline. "Well, make certain you stay away from the card rooms. Society here is nothing but one vast casino. I would not have our dear Rowly's sister drawn into the evils of this place. I daresay you have come for the waters and will find them quite invigorating; but the rest is an unending pursuit of pleasure occupying the whole day, to the exclusion of anything useful or sensible."

Many of the company gave unintelligible murmurs as the Countess paused for a sip of water. Then she continued, "All here is a tedious circle of unmeaning hurry, anxiety, fatigue, and fancied enjoyments the entire day. In short," she directly addressed Mary and Sarah, "nothing can be more trifling than the life of a lady nor," turning to Roger and Westmoreland, "more insipid than that of a gentleman at Bath. The one is a constant series of flirting and gadding about, the other of sauntering from place to place, without

42

any scheme or pursuit. Scandal and fashions engross the entire of conversations." Now she looked at Mrs. Tudway. "You and your party will, of course, choose a higher way of life, but you must be on your guard. The evil is insidious."

Mrs. Tudway offered a reassuring answer for the company.

Lady Selina gave Mary a pleasant smile. "Would you care to take a turn around the room? Colonel Hastings will escort us." Mary agreed, and the handsome uniformed man sitting on Selina's left instantly rose, held their chairs, and offered an arm to each lady. As the rest of the company was engrossed in conversation—or more particularly, in listening to the Countess who dismissed the three with a brief nod—Selina and Mary were left to a leisurely stroll around the room.

"Have you been in Bath long?" Lady Selina asked.

"We arrived only yesterday."

"And are you enjoying it?"

After the Countess' blunt words, Mary wasn't sure what she should reply. She didn't want Lady Selina to think her lost to all sense of propriety. "It is very beautiful."

"Indeed it is. And do not let Mama frighten you. You will find many delightful pastimes, though what she says about the vices is quite true. You must attend a service in our chapel when you have time. Mama is preparing a great celebration for the seventh anniversary of its opening. Rowland Hill—he would be your brother-in-law, would he not?—has preached there several times for Mama."

Mary was stunned. "Rowly? But he isn't ordained yet."

"No, and of course he doesn't celebrate Communion. But Mama has a seminary in Wales and she often offers opportunities for students to bring addresses in her chapel. Rowland Hill is the best I've ever heard. I believe he will be as great a preacher as Mr. Whitefield. There are even those who say Whitefield's mantle has fallen on him."

And again all Mary could say was, "Rowly?"

They continued their turn around the room and Mary was glad to see the tête-a-tête at the Countess' table was concluding when they arrived, because she had in no wise adjusted to Bath hours and at home would have breakfasted long ago.

Since the concert breakfasts were esteemed as some of the politest entertainments of the city, the Countess consented to be included in Westmoreland's party, and so the entire company took to their carriages to make the trip back up the hill to the Upper Rooms on Bennett Street off the Circus. The Upper Assembly Rooms, opened just the year before, had been designed by John Wood the Younger at the staggering sum of twenty thousand pounds, and now served as the center of the social life of the city.

Breakfast was set in the main ballroom, the tables and chairs dwarfed beneath the magnificent high ceiling. The pale blue room with its white plaster ornamentation and row of crystal chandeliers seemingly suspended in midair, seemed to Mary the most beautiful she'd ever seen. From the musicians' gallery, the orchestra filled the room with baroque music as ornamented as the architecture itself. Westmoreland explained to Mrs. Tudway that the breakfasts benefiting the orchestra were so popular that more funds were raised than needed, and the surplus was presented to the General Hospital.

With the abundance of fashionable company, beautiful music, and delectable food, it was easy to understand why these events were so popular. The menu was an elaborate affair of three courses of boiled and roasted meats, savory pies, and the famed Bath buns chock full of currants and with sticky icing that required licking of the fingers after eating.

But the Countess did not approve of the menu. "I never cease to be amazed by the folly of men who, realizing that without health life is a burden, and that this blessing can only be obtained by exercise and abstinence; yet, even after the heyday of youth is passed, will go on loading their bodies with distemper, pain, and sorrow, till life is not worth accepting, and then repair to Bath where they drink three pints of the Bath waters, and then sit down to a meal of hot spongy rolls, rendered high by burnt butter. Such a meal few young men in full health can get over without feeling much inconvenience, and I have known it to produce almost instantaneous death to valetudinarians."

In perhaps an attempt to mollify her ladyship, or at least to change the topic, Roger, who was enjoying his third such roll "high with burnt butter" said, "May I have the honor of escorting those of you who wish to attend to the Abbey for Matins? My uncle is to read the service. Dreadful bore, I fear, but one must do one's duty."

The Countess and her party had had morning prayers hours before in her private chapel; and Mrs. Tudway declined, as she

44

was to have her first meeting with Mr. Gainsborough that day; but Elizabeth agreed to accompany them, and Mrs. Child felt her presence would provide quite sufficient chaperonage for Sarah. So the smaller party arranged themselves in Westmoreland's elegant town coach and made the journey back down Milsom, Old Bond, and Stall Street to the Abbey, just a few steps across the courtyard from the Pump Room where they had met earlier.

Mary caught her breath as she entered the Abbey. The majestic view of the long nave, sweeping under the lacelike vaulting of the pale gold stone arches up to the brilliant stained-glass window with the midday sun behind it, was awe-inspiring.

"Pray, hurry along, Mary. We want to get the best seats." Sarah interrupted her reverie.

On Roger Twysden's arm, Mary walked the full length of the nave to the front seats reserved for members of the bishop's family. To the left of the altar sat the visiting Bishop on his throne, splendid in a surplice of finest lawn and lace mantle. The light from the jeweled window fell across his mitred head and added a glow to the expression of ineffable benediction on his face.

Looking around her, Mary saw that the Abbey was almost filled. And the worshipers nearly rivaled the gorgeous east window for richness of color and design. Everyone was clad in silk or satin, ornamented with gold or silver lace, metallic embroidery, and silk flounces. The towering headdresses of the women and powdered wigs of the men seemed to be reaching toward the gothic arches above them. But if the congregation's coiffures were reaching heavenward, that was the only part of them that did, as the elderly settled into comfortable sleep with their hands folded across their laps, and the young people flirted, the girls behind fluttering fans.

At first, Mary was shocked at such behavior in church; but when Roger winked at her in a way that made his blue-green eyes dance and she responded by fluttering her own fan, she decided it was all quite natural. Surely God wanted people to be happy in church.

The organ prelude came to an end and the Bishop rose and walked to the reading stand. In somber, melodious tones to rival that of the organ, he read from the prayer book. "Dearly beloved brethren, the Scripture moveth us in sundry places to acknowledge and confess our manifold sins and wickedness; and that we should not dissemble nor cloak them before the face of Almighty God our Heavenly Father; but confess them with an humble, lowly, penitent, and obedient heart. . . ."

Mary slipped to her knees with the rest of the congregation for the General Confession, the rich solemnity of the Bishop's voice making her think seriously of her own shortcomings and her need to seek forgiveness. "Almighty and most merciful Father; we have erred, and strayed from Thy ways like lost sheep. We have followed too much the devices and desires of our own hearts. . . ." Mary was repeating the words as her own prayer when she became aware of a nudging from Roger behind her. She opened her eyes and saw he was holding out a note to her. In some surprise she took the folded square of paper and opened it while the Bishop was reading the Absolution.

TO MARY

> Your eyes are as blue as the sky of Bath,
> Your voice as sweet as the bells in their spire,
> We met but this morn and already you hath
> Captured my heart; you my rapture inspire.

Confusion reigned in Mary's mind. Should she be flattered by Roger's attentions or outraged by his audacity? Was he so overcome by passion for her he couldn't restrain himself, or had he no more sense of propriety than to pass such a note during holy service? And then she became aware of the company around her. She had focused on the beauty of the service and had truly worshiped, as she always did in church; but even as the Bishop was reading, ". . . and grant that the rest of our life hereafter may be pure, and holy; so that at the last we may come to His eternal joy; through Jesus Christ our Lord," she heard giggles, sighs, whispers, all around her. Out of the corner of her eye she saw other notes being passed, even across the wide Abbey aisle.

So Roger was merely trifling with her, writing some flattering words—in bad verse—to pass the boredom of listening to his uncle. Her temper flared, and taking the prayer book from the rack in front of her, she brought it down with a sharp crack across his knuckles; she was only sorry that she couldn't bring it down on his head.

But, as always, her temper died as quickly as it flared and left her horrified at what she had done. Everyone must be staring. Her

46

mother would hear of it and she would be borne back to Wells in disgrace. Roger would be humiliated and never speak to her again. The first poem she received in Bath would be her last.

Then she looked up and saw Roger grinning at her saucily. And she realized that there had been no cessation of activity around her. All were so intent on their own flirtations that even Sarah and Westmoreland beside her had not noticed what she had done. And then she heard a similar sharp crack behind her and knew that another lady had rapped her suitor's knuckles with a fan. Mary's flare of temper had led her to act, though in sincerity, as any lady of fashion would have in teasing.

Still confused by the topsy-turvy values of the society in which she found herself, Mary returned Roger's smile. But after the service, she declined his invitation to escort her to the bookseller's. She really wanted to be alone for a while to think.

The beauty and order of the house in the Royal Crescent welcomed her; and her room, serene with its green and white striped wallpaper, gold-draped white French bed, and silk-skirted dressing table, was the perfect place to attempt to order her thoughts. Even in one day she could see that Bath offered the amusement she sought; but how did she reconcile this to the values of her home in Wells?

If she must choose among the stolid boredom of a country life, the charming but superficial pleasures of the fashionable world, or the long-faced religion of an enthusiast like the Countess of Huntingdon, it all seemed a rather hopeless lot. But her frown turned to a smile as she thought of the humorous moments of the past twenty hours, and she wished that Rowland could have been there to share her amusement. At the same time, she was glad he wasn't. What would he think of the company she had chosen?

In the days that followed, Mary had little time for reflection. With Roger as her constant companion, she became well acquainted with his uncle the Bishop, who was a close friend of Mrs. Child. Any time a doubt prickled her mind as to the propriety of attitudes she heard expressed by the bright company Sarah Child gathered around herself and her constant companion, the Earl, Mary could readily salve her conscience with the thought that, after all, a Bishop was one of their company.

The only real cloud to her happiness appeared the following week when she and Elizabeth returned from making the rounds of

47

shops in Milsom Street, with two footmen carrying parcels of the finest of spangle-embroidered fans, kid gloves, silk mesh mittens, and satin ribbons.

"Oh!" Elizabeth picked up the post Benson had placed on the hall table. "A letter from Jane! I haven't heard news of Hawkstone for such ages. Come to my room, Mary, and let me share it with you. Send up a tea tray, Benson."

But as soon as Mary and Elizabeth had removed their hats and gloves and were sipping dishes of the finest Hyson tea, Elizabeth opened her letter and her face fell. "Mary, I fear the news is not good. Jane has received a letter from our Rowland. He has been much in the furnace these past weeks."

Mary instantly felt a pang of shame for the mindless gaiety of her past days while her friend had been suffering.

"Jane has copied out part of Rowland's letter. Shall I read it to you?" Mary nodded, her eyes wide with interest.

"The Master said I might stay in University provided I would not disturb the town by public conventicles; and would also give him a promise not to teach in the University any doctrine contrary to the Thirty-Nine Articles. To the former, I answered I had no intention of doing so, as I had told him before; and tho I could safely give him a promise to the latter in the absolute, if he really meant that I should not talk about religion to the gownsmen, as I supposed he did, I could make no such promise."

Elizabeth paused for a sip of tea. "I cannot bear to think what it will mean if he is forced to leave the University just two months before degrees are awarded. It would be a disaster for Rowland, but it would kill our parents. Such a thing is unthinkable."

She picked up the letter, read a bit in silence, then put it down again with a sigh. "More bad news. The authorities at Oxford have expelled six undergraduates who believe as Rowland does, but did not so much as preach publicly. What will Cambridge do to one so outspoken as our brother? I tried to warn him when I saw him at Wells. He must give this up! Enthusiasm in religion is social suicide."

Mary nodded unhappily. She had spoken to Bishop Twysden on the subject in the Pump Room only that morning—in veiled terms, of course, not so as to let him known that a connection of hers embraced such a doctrine. The Bishop had been amused and outraged at the very mention of the subject. "Madmen, the lot of them. Believe we are all sinners and God will punish us. Such ideas won't hold today. Much too enlightened for that. Of course it's in the prayer book, but that's just tradition; nobody really listens to it."

Mary took a long sip of tea. Who was right? Rowland was prepared to put his entire career and future success on the line for his faith. The Countess had devoted her life and private fortune to just such an enthusiasm. Yet, who should be a better guide in spiritual matters than a Bishop? Sarah was perfectly happy without any notions of a personal God. Roger was a delightful companion of the first fashion, and as the nephew of a Bishop, he surely had proper instructions in all matters of the church.

And what difference did it all make anyway? She had been baptized as an infant, confirmed when she was twelve, and had attended services regularly, with more devotion than most. Surely that was sufficient. If poor Rowland was determined to be pigheaded, she would simply have to consign him to his own perdition. Other than listening to Elizabeth's worries, it needn't affect her. What did it matter to her what Elizabeth's brother chose to do?

· 4 ·

AT CAMBRIDGE, STILL AWAITING the fateful decision of the Master of his college, Rowland was convinced that a spiritual decision was the one that mattered most in life; and that such a matter of faith and conscience in which he was being tested was indeed worth staking all his future. That Sunday he had preached to a small village congregation in nearby Barton; now he wrestled with the matter of explaining his position to his sister Jane.

But before he could put his thoughts into words, he reviewed the letters of encouragement from George Whitefield. He was thankful that he had kept the four letters from the great preacher. Since Whitefield's death in America two years earlier, he had been sorely missed by the thousands of people he had helped on both sides of the Atlantic.

The first letter was written several years before when the conflict began, but it was as if Whitefield had foreseen the very situation Rowland was facing.

About thirty-four years ago, the master of Pembroke College, where I was educated, took me to task for visiting the sick and going to the prisons. In my haste I said, "Sir, if it displeaseth you, I will go no more;" my heart smote me immediately—I repented and went again. He heard of it, threatened, but for fear he should be looked upon as a persecutor, let me alone. The hearts of all are in the Redeemer's hands. I would not have you give way, no, not for a moment. The storm is too great to hold long. Visiting the sick and imprisoned, and instructing the ignorant are the very vitals of true and undefiled religion. If threatened, denied degree, or expelled for *this*, it will be the best degree you can take. A glorious preparative for, and a blessed presage of, future usefulness. Now is your time to prove the strength of Jesus yours.

Blind as he is, Satan sees some great good coming on. We never prospered so much at Oxford as when we were hissed at and reproached as we walked along the street. It is a poor building that a little stinking breath of Satan's vassals can throw down. Your house I trust is better founded—is it not built upon a rock? Is not that rock the blessed Jesus? The gates of hell, therefore, shall not be able to prevail against it. Go on, therefore, my dear Man, go on; old Berridge, I believe, would give you the same advice; you are honored in sharing Christ's reproach and name.

God bless and direct and support you—He will, He will. Good Lady Huntingdon is in town—you will not lack her prayers.

Yours, &c. &c.
In an all-conquering Jesus,

G.W.

To Mr. Rowland Hill
St. John's College, Cambridge

Yes, Whitefield was right. Rowland didn't doubt a word of his letter. But how could he make his family see this? How explain to his mother and father that it would be a *good* thing to be expelled for conscience' sake? And Mary—would she ever speak to him again if he presented himself to her sans degree, sans ordination? He had been so sure when last he spoke to her at The Cedars and hinted so broadly of what was in his heart. What would his great stand for conscience' sake mean to her?

He turned to his second letter from Whitefield. Its assurance about his family was just what Rowland needed.

I have had a profitable conference with your brother Richard. He tells me your brother Brian may soon be gained for the

Kingdom. What grace is this! Who knows but the root as well as the branches may be taken by and by: Abba, Father, all things are possible with Thee. Steadiness and perseverance in the children will be one of the best means, under God, of convincing the parents. Their present opposition I think cannot last very long; if it does, to obey God rather than man, when forbidden to do what is undoubted duty, is the invariable rule.

Satan sees he is only a mastiff chained. Continue to inform me how he barks, and how far he is permitted to go in your parts; and God's people shall be more and more stirred up to pray for you all.

Yours, &c. &c.
In our all-conquering Emmanuel,

G.W.

To Mr. Rowland Hill,
At Hawkstone, Shropshire.

If only Whitefield's prophecy might come true, that his parents would see the light. But so far there was no sign of it. At the sound of a knock on his outer door, Rowland put the letters away and rose. Why did he always feel a sense of dread these days when an unexpected caller came by? If this kept up much longer, he would soon be as long-faced as Bottisham. But he relaxed when he saw his old friends Pentycross, Simpson, and Robinson.

"Come to escort you to the Greek Testament lecture, old man. You look as though you could use some help." Pentycross greeted.

"Egad, is it six o'clock already?" Rowland hurried back to his inner room to throw on his black academical robe and grab the soft black cap required for lectures. "Been looking over Whitefield's letters."

"Oh, yes," Pentycross said. "I remember the verse he sent me when my exhibition was withdrawn, for visiting the sick and such.

> Satan thwarts and men object;
> Yet the thing they thwart, effect."

"And so it is with you, eh, Penty?" Simpson said.

"Yes, I have continued quite well without their grant of thirty pounds a year. And Frampton told me later it was hearing the story of my steadfastness that brought him into our society. Would that I had thirty thousand to give up for Jesus' sake."

"Hear, hear!" Robinson said with a raised fist, as they crossed the courtyard to the lecture hall.

This lecture which the vice-provost conducted at a sacrifice of his day of rest, was the great college concession to the idea that young ordinands should be given some background in the Holy Scripture; it purported to be a critical and exegetical analysis of the Gospels. The students were asked to construe a passage from St. Matthew or St. John, and occasionally the vice-provost would read from some commentator, offering an explanation of the text.

Rowland would have infinitely preferred quiet reading in his own rooms, or a study time with his friends, especially as few, other than his circle, attended the lecture with clear heads. He felt the lecture did rather more harm than good, for there always arose a wine-gathering after Hall on Sundays and a great deal of wine was consumed in a very short time on the plea, "We've no time to lose, so pass the wine." And the wine was passed. Rowland had accepted an invitation to only one such party, but it served as an adequate education as to why scarcely any of the gownsmen were sedate enough to enter into the meaning of the lecture.

The week wore on with similarly unprofitable lectures. Rowland chafed at the enforced curtailment of his activities, but was grateful for the loopholes that allowed him to visit the sick beyond Cambridge and to preach at the Castle. Of course, if the authorities had thought of those things, they would have forbidden them also, but for the moment he could continue. At times he wished for the final blow. If the decision came on the side of expelling him, then he would be released from all bounds by the college and he could preach wherever anyone would listen to him.

But when Pearce presented himself in Rowland's rooms, it was merely to inquire into his charge's studies. He had no news of his own to deliver.

"Pearce, you're a good fellow to carry this brief for me. But I am wearied with the waiting. I believe I should beard the Master in his den myself. I feel such a coward hiding behind my tutor's skirts."

"It's nothing of the kind, Hill. The Master has chosen to operate in this fashion and we must be content. If you were to go to him yourself, he would merely see it as another infraction of the rules."

And so Rowland waited. The one bright spot of those weary days was a letter from the Countess of Huntingdon inviting him to attend the celebration of the seventh anniversary of the opening of her chapel in Bath the following month. "Our dear Charles Wesley will lead the music, and our old friends Romaine and Fletcher have promised their attendance. I have hopes of Berridge. If only Whitefield were here to preach again as he did at the opening. But we must carry on apace. I shall expect you."

Well, if he were not allowed to remain in Cambridge, his time would be his own. But even if he did complete his degree, there would be time for a visit to Bath at Eastertime. And if the Master's decision was negative, he would not likely be welcome at Hawkstone; so all round it was a cheering prospect. Except that in her last letter, Elizabeth informed him that Mary and Mrs. Tudway had accompanied her to Bath. If Mary were still in the city at Easter, it could mean only a renewal of the argument they had not concluded at The Cedars. He had so hoped that when he saw Mary again, he would come to her complete with his degree and ordination—solid credentials which would put an end to her pleas that he give up his irregular preaching. When fully ordained, he would not need to hold irregular services. "Lord, speed the day," was his heartfelt prayer, as he thought of all that ordination meant to his future. But he must have his degree first.

The last Saturday in March was mild and sunny with clumps of daffodils and crocus blooming on the Backs of the colleges along the river, and a soft spring green frosting the fields, fens, and hedgerows beyond Cambridge. This would be a perfect day to call on his old mentor, John Berridge.

The ride to Everton did much to restore Rowland's humor which had been sorely tried of late. He even found himself singing as he rode the last few miles to the vicarage at Everton. His youthful reading of Dr. Watt's hymns for children had awakened his earliest religious impressions, and he always found recalling that experience a boost to his spirits.

Just outside the village, however, he stopped singing to observe an interesting sight. A butcher, proclaimed so by his heavy, blood-stained apron and the square cap on his head, was marching straight for his shop, with a trail of five fine cows following him.

There was no driver behind with a whip, and the butcher didn't even look behind to make sure the cattle were following. Rowland reigned in his horse and sat a moment, observing. What secret did this pied piper possess that the cows would follow him to slaughter so docilely of their own free will?

At last he spotted a clue and, laughing, spurred his horse. At the old stone vicarage, he tossed his reins over the post and bounded forward. Berridge, who had seen him coming, threw open the door and stood with arms outstretched, a broad smile wreathing his round face.

"My dear Rowly, my very dear Rowly, what a joyous surprise! I see by your demeanor that you bring me good news."

Rowland clasped his friend's hands. "Indeed, I bring you excellent news. I have just discovered a new illustration for a sermon."

"Well, come in, come in, and tell me." The white-haired man led the way into his book-lined study.

"As I was coming along, I saw a butcher followed by a number of cattle. I couldn't at first make out how he got them to follow him. But presently I saw that he dropped some beans as he went along, and the animals picked them up and ate them. Thus he got them into the slaughterhouse and closed the door." Rowland thumped on Berridge's desk as if on a pulpit. "This, I say, is just what the devil does to lead sinners. They must be warned before the door is slammed on them."

Berridge threw back his head and laughed. "My dear Rowly, a most excellent example, indeed. But have you come to tell me that you have been permitted to preach?"

The pleasant, springtime ride, the joy of singing his favorite childhood songs, and the unexpected thrill of finding new sermon material had put Rowland's troubles completely out of his mind, But now they were back. He sank into a chair. "Alas, no, Sir. I have not. There is no news. The Master delays, and Pearce tells me there is nothing more I can do but to behave with circumspection and attend lectures. It is exceedingly chafing."

Berridge nodded, his face serious, except for the perennial twinkle in his eyes. "Yes, it chafes. When I was a Fellow at Clare Hall, Cambridge, I was surrounded with witty and amusing companions such as you well know the University abounds in. But when I 'turned Methodistical,' I too found the jeers and opprobrium indeed chafed. And I can see by the glow your little anecdote brought over you that preaching is your all-in-all."

Berridge rang a small bell on the table by his chair and when his housekeeper appeared, he requested a tea tray—a hearty one to refresh his young friend. Then he turned back to Rowland. "Luther used to say that when the Lord had fresh work for him, a strong trial was sent beforehand to prepare him for it by humiliation. So take these present slings and arrows as precursors of God's blessings."

Rowland started to speak, but was hindered by the entrance of Mrs. Stoke, with a repast of cold meat, cheese, and jellies. Rowland found he was indeed hungry—the hungriest he had been for days.

"Eat up, my dear Rowly. And listen well. What better bargain can you find than to fill your stomach and your mind at the same time?" Berridge took a sip of tea, well laced with milk and sugar, then continued his homily. "Study not to be a fine preacher. Jerichos are blown down with rams' horns. Look simply unto Jesus for preaching food and what is wanted will be given; and what is given will be blessed, whether it be a barley or a wheaten loaf, a crust or a crumb." He paused to push Mrs. Stoke's basket of buns closer to Rowland. "Your mouth will be a flowing stream, or a fountain sealed, according as your heart is. Avoid all controversy in preaching, talking, or writing; preach nothing down but the devil, and nothing up but Jesus Christ."

Rowland shook his head with a rueful smile. "Avoid all controversy! You cannot know how I should like to follow your advice. But controversy follows me as the tail follows the dog. It seems the only way I can avoid controversy is by avoiding preaching. And if I am to do that, I had as well quit breathing."

"No, no, you must not do that. Breathe deeply. But breathe of His spirit. I think your chief work for a season will be to break up fallow ground. This suits the accents of your voice at present. God will give you other use of your tongue when it is wanted; but now He sends you out to thrash the mountains, and a glorious thrashing it is. Go forth, my dear Rowly, whenever you are invited into the devil's territories; carry the Redeemer's standard along with you and blow the gospel trumpet boldly, fearing nothing but yourself. If you meet with success, as I trust you will, expect clamor and threats from the world, and a little venom now and then from its children. These bitter herbs make good sauce for a young recruiting sergeant, whose heart would be lifted up with pride if it were not kept down by these pressures."

Berridge refilled his guest's cup. "The more success you meet with, the more opposition you will find; but Jesus sitteth above the waterfloods and remaineth a King forever. His eye is ever upon you, and His heavenly guards surround you. Therefore, fear not; go on humbly, go on boldly, trusting only in Jesus, and all opposition shall fall before you. Make the Scriptures your only study, and be much in prayer. The apostles gave themselves to the Word of God and to prayer. Do thou likewise."

Rowland had been listening with pleasure to the words of his spiritual guide, drinking them in, savoring them, and showing his agreement with a slight nod of his head. But suddenly Berridge took a new tack. "Now is your time to work for Jesus; you have health and youth on your side, and no church or wife on your back."

Rowland could not keep the frown from his face, and his cup clattered in its saucer. "Ah, I see that I have touched a sore spot." Berridge laughed. "You are thinking that now I have ceased preaching and gone to meddling."

"As things now stand, it appears unlikely that I shall ever, as you say, 'have a wife on my back.' But I do not view that as a happy state of affairs. Preaching is my all-in-all, in that it is *first*, but it is not quite *all* that is in my heart."

Berridge was serious now. "Indeed, I am sorry to hear it. Very sorry. Grieved even. Have you not read St. Paul's advice on the subject? I am unalterably opposed to the marriage of our young Methodist clergy. Those who will try it have been punished for their folly. Charles Wesley was spoilt for his work by his happy marriage. John Wesley and George Whitefield were only saved from making shipwreck of the cause by God's sending them a pair of ferrets for wives."

Even on a subject so near his heart, Rowland could not resist an attempt at levity. "It is your advice then, that if I must marry I should take a shrew for a wife?"

But Berridge, who could seldom resist a joke, saw this as no laughing matter. "How many a minister we have seen who in early life was active, zealous, and useful, who, when settled as pastor and united in wedlock to an amiable and agreeable woman, became—if not entirely negligent—at least comparatively indifferent and useless to the work. The attractions of domestic life are powerful; the spirit of the world creeps in, the strength of personal piety lessens, and he becomes—alas, for himself and others—at ease in Zion."

The conversation turned to happier subjects while Rowland finished Mrs. Stoke's repast. He then took his leave, for he had a long ride before him.

And much to think about on his ride. Was Berridge right? Even if he could persuade Mary to become his bride, would it spell disaster for his ministry? Perhaps his lack of success in wooing her was God's answer for the pattern his life was to take. If this were so, he should rejoice in her indifference to him. But he could not do so.

Later in the week, when his long-awaited answer came from the Master's lodge, he found it further complicated the matter of his love for Mary.

The warmth and scent of spring filled the air and Rowland had no desire to return to his room or visit the library after lecture, so he continued on across tiny Third Court which was squeezed between Second Court and the river, and walked across Kitchen Bridge, the stone structure designed by Sir Christopher Wren in the previous century. The Backs were landscaped with walks, a bowling green, carefully trimmed hedges, and a wilderness bounded by a yew hedge. Rowland was strolling along one of the gravel paths, considering following it to the fields beyond, when Pearce's voice calling his name made him turn round to the river.

"Hill, I say, Hill. I have word at last."

As both men were long-legged and rapid of stride, they were together in an instant. Pearce didn't even wait for Rowland to voice his questions. "I have purchased for you a peg tower. I have assurance all will be amicably settled. You will receive your degree."

"And what are the terms fixed upon?" Rowland was careful not to claim victory before he knew the terms of surrender, or indeed, which side had surrendered.

"In the end, the Master was exceedingly vague. Never a word was mentioned of your visiting the sick and imprisoned, dispensing Methodistical books, or of frequenting houses suspected of Methodism."

"In short, I am free to do just what I please!" Now Rowland would permit himself to rejoice. "I perceive that the Master only wanted to draw his head out of the halter as handsomely as he could. Blessed be God!" He grabbed Pearce's hand and pumped it up and down vigorously, but Pearce was too much the dutiful tutor to give himself over entirely to celebration. He could not consider his commission complete without a sturdy word of warning. "And now that this matter is successfully concluded that you may remain for your degree, may I suggest that you put all other matters out of your mind but the successful completion of your work? We have but one term left now to prepare for exams and orders!"

"Indeed, Pearce." Rowland was still shaking his hand. "Indeed. I shall be entirely at your command—after vacation. I go to Bath next week. Then my brain shall be all yours for the term, to cram as much learning into it as your heart desires."

At last Pearce extracted his hand from Rowland's large grip and turned toward the library. To his surprise, Rowland accompanied him. "I had thought my news might send you off on one of your famous swims or out to gather a crowd to preach to."

Rowland looked longingly at the river sparkling in the afternoon sun. "Alas, there are those whose concern over this matter has been greater than my own. I must write to my sister Jane."

But the task was more difficult than he anticipated. Such happy news should have come tumbling out on the paper before him; but as Rowland sat in St. John's library with dark wooden shelves of books running up to the ceiling on three sides of him, the narrow space filled with birdsong from the open window and the splash and plod of barge horses pulling their loads up the Cam just beyond the window, he found it hard to discipline his thoughts into words. He dipped his pen and tried again.

My Very Dear Sister,

Cambridge, Tuesday

I am ashamed that I have been so long in writing; but I thought you would like to hear from me when all things were settled. I have met with delivery from the Master's clutches. He commissioned my tutor to meet with me and to tell me that *I might stay*.

The town and University are entirely surrendered to my episcopal visitation *a prelate*. My only grief is that for the present I am in a great measure an unpreaching prelate. However, this unmixed mercy will soon be remedied. My remarkably kind tutor tells me he has not the least doubt but that I may be ordained next May. How wonderfully this is ordered! Tis well the government is upon Jesus' shoulders, tho my rebellious heart thought very hard of so many seemingly reverse providences in the past. I must learn by experience that glorious song, "Worthy Is the Lamb."

I prepare now to go to Bath for our good Lady Huntingdon's celebration.

For this reason excuse the haste of this from your poor unworthy Br.

Ro Hill

But the last line to Jane brought directly over his head the small dark cloud that had been following him for days. For a moment he could have thought the sound of splashing water from the river was rain on his spirits.

He had won his hard-fought battle. He had stood strong on matters of conscience, and authority had capitulated. There now appeared no barrier to achieving all he most fervently desired: degree, ordination, Mary.

He should have been full of joy at the thought that he would see Mary next week, especially now that he had good news to bring her. But Berridge's solemn exhortation was heavy on his mind. . . . "Unalterably opposed to marriage . . . those who try it have been punished for their folly . . . alas for himself and others, he becomes at ease in Zion."

He had always assumed that his longstanding fondness for Mary, coming about so naturally through family connections and fired by her personal charms, had been of God's directing. But if Berridge was right, far from being a bounteous blessing, his tender feeling for Mary must be regarded as a temptation, an ensnaring trap to be avoided at the peril of his soul.

· 5 ·

"BUT WHY SHOULD I GO to the baths when I am not ill?" Mary asked Sarah a few days later, as they strolled across the courtyard that was the heart of Bath, linking as it did the Abbey, the Pump Room, and the King's Bath. The two ladies and their escorts, the ever-present Roger and Westmoreland, paused to look over the stone wall surrounding the largest and most popular of the city's five public baths. Several of their fellow promenaders had likewise paused to observe the bathers bobbing in the steamy air of the mineral water pool—an activity that had made Bath a popular resort since first it was enjoyed by Roman legions, who found the hot waters a sometime substitute for the balmy Mediterranean.

Mary looked up at the arched windows of the Pump Room and observed a number of the promenaders there likewise watching the bathers. "If I am to bathe, I should prefer a less public place."

"Certainly. You must attend the Cross Bath just at the end of Bath Street. It is much more genteel," Roger said.

Sarah laughed. "Fah, Sir. Is such a description intended to tempt her? You make it sound a dreadful bore. Never fear, Mary. You will find it quite invigorating and much more a social event or a sport than a mere physician's prescription."

So the next morning Mary and Mrs. Tudway arrived at the Cross Bath with Sarah and Mrs. Child shortly after the popular hour of six. Since they were driven there in a closed carriage, they came attired in the regulation gowns made of a yellow canvaslike material.

"This scratches." Mary tugged at the square-cut neckline of

61

her bathing garment.

"Never mind. It will feel more comfortable in the water. And it's quite necessary—it would be most unfortunate to go into the water in a garment that clung to one's form when wet."

Mary shuddered at the idea and tucked a linen handkerchief into her chipstraw bonnet, as she had been warned she would need it to wipe the perspiration from her face. A woman attendant came forward to lead them down the stairs into the water and presented each of them with a little floating dish containing confections, a handkerchief, and a vial of perfume. The attendant stayed with the older ladies, but Sarah and Mary chose to traverse the bath by themselves, pushing along their black lacquered trays.

The great billowing sleeves and skirts of their garments filled with water and Mary giggled. "Oh, I shall be bobbing like a cork in a moment. Pray, hold my hand, Sarah, so that I won't be borne off."

"Will my hand do?" asked a familiar masculine voice.

Mary splashed the water in her surprise, making Roger cry out in protest. "Egad, if you wish me to take my leave, just say so. No need to drown me."

"But I thought, that is, I had heard—" Mary was confused by this unexpected turn. "I had supposed the sexes were kept separate in this bath," she finished.

"Yes, I believe there was some fusty notion of that," Roger said, and presented her with a nosegay of fragrant violets and lily of the valley. "But no one pays it any heed. No more so than any other of the Beau's Rules of the Bath."

"Indeed," Westmoreland said. "But this one is honored in the breach, while the others are simply no longer necessary as matters of enforcement."

"Such as?" Sarah asked, sniffing prettily at her nosegay from Westmoreland, then setting it afloat, its pink and violet ribbons drifting in the water.

"Such as that no man or woman should go into any bath, by day or night, without a decent covering on their bodies, under the penalty of three shillings and fourpence. Or that no person shall presume to cast or throw any dog or other live beast into any of the said baths, under the like penalty of three shillings and fourpence. And that no person shall thrust, cast, or throw another into any of the said baths with his or her clothes on, under a penalty of six shillings and eightpence."

Laughing at Rapid Westmoreland's account of the regulations, they made their way to the far end of the pool, past the bath's namesake, a large stone cross in the center of the water which stood as a memorial to the consort of James II who had been cured by the waters. "Indeed," Mary said, "I'm most grateful to Mr. Nash. I shouldn't find it at all pleasant to bathe with dogs or other beasts." And she thought it not unpleasant that any prohibition against mixed bathing had gone uninforced. The men looked most handsome, clad in breeches and waistcoats from the familiar yellow canvas with their tricorn hats on their powered hair. But that observation made her think of her own appearance and she dabbed lightly at her glowing face with the handkerchief from her bowl.

From the stone-arched gallery along the side of the bath, an orchestra began playing and the idle visitors who had gathered to watch the bathers applauded. Mary would have been more comfortable without the gallery viewers, but the bath was as invigorating as Sarah had promised.

Roger, noting her uneasy glance at the gallery, leaned close to her ear. "The bath is most becoming to you, my Dear. You can be assured that no man who has seen you here would part with you for the best mermaid in Christendom."

Mary found Roger's words about her appearance reassuring, and any misgivings she might have had at his meaning were forgotten, as they all laughed at Westmoreland's quotation of the popular couplet,

> And today many persons of rank and condition
> Were boiled by command of an able physician.

Not to be outdone by his friend's poetry, Roger sprang to the side of the pool and struck an antic posture, balancing on one foot like a statue; then, pretending to lose his balance, he teetered dangerously on the edge and plunged into the water, showering the ladies with drops of water. Then he bobbed to the surface, floating on his back, and gazed up into Mary's face. "Ah, what rapture! It is Neptune's ladylove I see! Ah, Fair Damsel, take me, take me!" He held out his arms to embrace the elements and sank in rapture to the accompaniment of the ladies' laughter.

How long such acrobatics might have continued they were not to

63

know, for Mrs. Child sent an attendant to inform them that she was ready to leave the bath.

The rest of the morning passed with its pleasant occupations, and that afternoon, as had become their habit, the gentlemen escorted Sarah and Mary to the shops.

On the way up Milsom Street toward the bookroom, they passed by a coffeehouse designated for ladies; gentlemen read the papers in another establishment across the way. Sarah looked longingly at the ladies of fashion entering their meeting place. "Alas, I should like to attend there someday. But my mama says young girls are not admitted, insomuch as the conversation turns upon politics, scandal, philosophy, and other subjects above our capacity. I think it sounds far more interesting than the fusty old bookseller I was obliged to subscribe to for a crown and a quarter."

"In truth, Miss Child," Westmoreland said, tapping his walking stick on the cobbled walk, "I can warrant that you miss nothing in passing by the forbidden fruit. In your Office of Intelligence, all the reports of the day and all the private transactions of the Bath are discussed as fully as in any other room."

The men stood aside at the door to allow the ladies to enter first, and Mary could not help but feel flattered by the warmth of Roger's admiring glances as she folded her parasol and walked before him. She knew she looked her best in her cream silk polonaise gown with the overskirt of its Chinese pattern in pink and green caught up in draped puffs at the back. But as she went up the stairs she could not help blushing as she felt his gaze upon her ankle, made visible by the shorter French style.

As they entered, the Abbey bells pealed forth, announcing the arrival of someone of importance—probably a member of the aristocracy, from the length of the ring. Sarah led the way directly to a table already occupied by a set of her acquaintances who were deep in gossip.

"They say Lady Lechmere lost above seven hundred pounds in one sitting at the gaming tables."

"Zounds, when Lord Lechmere hears of *this*—"

A gentleman accompanying the ladies took a pinch of snuff.

"It will be a wonder if all the sweetness the waters can put into Lord Lechmere's blood can make him endure it!"

"Then Miss Nunsworthy danced three times with Mr. Runstrete. When her guardian hears word of *that*, I shouldn't care to be responsible for the outcome."

The conversations continued, punctuated with peals of giggles and flutters of fans; but Mary soon wearied of the veiled innuendos and shredding of reputations. She rose and took a turn around the room, spending more time looking at the books on the tables than at the fashionable people pretending to read them. In spite of her desire for a gayer life that offered more diversion than she knew in Wells, Mary was by nature a quiet, peaceable person, not a meddler or a gossip.

"May I help you select a volume to your taste?" The ever-attentive Roger was by her side. "Do you prefer to read novels, plays, pamphlets, or newspapers?"

"Is there no poetry, Sir?"

"Ah, indeed, Milady." After making an excellent leg, he selected a small volume of Cavalier poetry and began reading to her as they strolled around the room.

> "Gather ye rosebuds while ye may,
>   Old Time is still a-flying!
> And this same flower that smiles to-day,
>   To-morrow will be dying. . . .
>
> That age is best which is the first
>   When youth and blood are warmer. . . .
>
> Then be not coy, but use your time:
>   And while ye may, go marry:
> For having lost but once your prime,
>   You may forever tarry."

The light verse was read in a charming manner. Mary, however, could not help thinking of the words. "It seems, Sir, that if time is short, the poet should urge people to make the most of it to accomplish something of value, not to fritter it away gathering rosebuds."

"Where did you come by such a graybeard notion? I find the poem excellent advice myself. One sees enough of the broken-down superannuated in the Pump Room to serve as a warning; now is the time to live for pleasure; another opportunity is unlikely to come." To add emphasis to his argument, he turned from Robert Herrick to the poetry of Thomas Carew.

"If the quick spirits in your eye
Now languish and anon must die;
If every sweet and every grace
Must fly from that forsaken face;
Then, Mary, let us reap our joys
Ere time such goodly fruit destroys."

She blushed at his insertion of her name in the poem and quickly changed the subject for fear he might pursue the innuendos. "I fear I must confess to preferring more thoughtful work—such as *Paradise Lost*. But I have of late begun reading novels. Mama says it is quite acceptable now that I am out. Mr. Fielding's books make me blush, but *The Castle of Oranto* gives me the most agreeable chills."

"Ah, indeed. You fancy Walpole's apparitions, do you—the giant in armor, a skeleton perambulating in a hermit's cowl, a statue that drips blood?"

Mary laughed. "Perhaps it is the chills that I enjoy more than the phantoms themselves."

"Allow me to select a novel for you." Roger paused before a bookcase on the wall. "Ah, I fancy you will find this to your liking. Smollett's *Humphrey Clinker*, written only last year and set largely right here in Bath. It is rumored he borrowed freely from Anstey's *New Bath Guide;* but be that as it may, it is quite a diverting work." He handed the bookseller two shillings for the volume and presented it to Mary.

Sarah and Westmoreland were still deep in gossip, so Roger offered to escort Miss Tudway back to the Royal Crescent.

Benson opened the door at their approach. "Mrs. Tudway—Mrs. Clement, that is—has a guest just arrived, Miss. She asked me to show you into the drawing room as soon as you returned."

"Oh?" Mary undid the ribbons on her round straw hat. "I didn't think Elizabeth would be back from her portrait sitting yet. A new arrival? How exciting. I heard the bells ring—were they for Elizabeth's guest?"

Mary was looking down, pulling off her white lutestring gloves as she entered the room, so she was fully in front of the visitor before she saw who it was. "Rowland! What a first-rate surprise! I

66

had not thought to see you for months yet."

As he rose she noted his handsome stature in his finely cut cinnamon coat, but something was amiss. The sparkle with which he always greeted her was gone. She took a step backward. "O Rowly. Do not tell me. You have been sent down! Oh, this is dreadful." Although she had warned him of the likelihood and could now have the pleasure of saying, "I told you so," she had not thought she would find the event so wounding.

Rowland bowed stiffly over her hand. "On the contrary, Mary. I appreciate your concern, if not your confidence, but I have just been informing my sister that the Master has consented that I may take my degree."

Before Mary could reply, Roger, who had remained in the entrance hall to give Benson his hat, gloves, and walking stick, entered.

Mary introduced the two men who acknowledged each other coolly. In an attempt to bridge the distance between them, she offered, "Mr. Twysden's uncle is a Bishop: undoubtedly you know of him, Rowland."

His reply was indistinct.

After paying his respects to Elizabeth, Roger told Mary he hoped to see her at the Assembly rooms that evening, and took his leave.

Mary turned to sit on the sofa beside Elizabeth, and Rowland went back to the Sheraton chair. She started to speak, but Rowland was first. "Is that fellow a proper person for you to know, Mary?"

Rowland's high-handed attitude made Mary's temper flare. "La, Sir. Are you to superintend me now that Miss Fossbenner has been dispensed with? I *told* you he is the nephew of a Bishop. And what have you to say to it if my mama approves?"

"You are quite right. Forgive me."

"Faith, Sir, that is much better." Mary smiled at him; her point won, her temper cooled. "Now, tell me, you have agreed to refrain from your irregular preaching?"

"No. The authorities made no such demands. Had they required me to act contrary to my conscience, I should have accepted expulsion rather than submit."

"Oh, lud! If you aren't the most starched-up person I have ever known. Why must you be so obdurate, so intractable, and—and so muleheaded?"

"Is that what I am? Indeed, I must apologize for my character. I had thought a stand upon principle admirable, but I see I mistook. I shall attempt to amend my ways. Perhaps a dose of the waters here would make me more wishy-washy." The sparkle had returned to his eyes.

And his amusement lighted her own. "How unhandsome of you to roast me, Sir, when I was merely giving you valuable advice."

"And how unjust of you to accuse me of grilling you when all I did was to agree with you."

As usual, Mary found that she couldn't maintain her irritation with Rowland above five minutes in his company, so she relaxed with the laughter she felt bubbling inside her and noted that the coldness she had felt directed toward herself when she first entered had thawed considerably.

To her surprise, Rowland rose a few minutes later to take his leave. "But aren't you staying here? I am certain Clement would wish you to," Elizabeth protested.

"No. I thank you, but I have accepted Lady Huntingdon's invitation. Since it is her celebration that brings me to Bath, it will be most convenient."

"Oh, indeed. The chapel is attached to her house, so you can pray ever so much more often." Mary could have bitten her tongue as soon as the words left her mouth. And her desire to recall them increased when she saw that the ice had returned to Rowland's countenance.

Elizabeth smoothed the situation. "Clement and I are getting up a party to attend the gala at Sydney Gardens tonight. Won't you join us, Rowly? I sent a card to Lady Selina and Colonel Hastings, so you could come in their carriage."

Rowland accepted his sister's invitation before bowing his farewell to the ladies.

Elizabeth turned to Mary. "And what of you, my Dear? Will you join our party tonight?"

For a moment Mary was tempted, then stiffened her resolve. Rowland must not think her softened to his nonconformist ideas. "Thank you, Elizabeth, but I have engaged to join the Child's party to the cotillion ball in the Upper Rooms." But as Elizabeth left her to see to the arrangements for the evening, Mary felt strangely depressed at the thought of the hours before her.

When she returned at eleven o'clock, with Roger's meaningful stares and sometimes ribald witticisms fresh in her mind, she was even more depressed. Especially when Elizabeth came in to inquire how she was, and went into raptures over the Gardens with their shady groves, grottoes, labyrinths, and waterfalls. "And the illuminations—quite marvelous how they contrive to light the trees and borders—gives the effect of giant fireflies, or of stars having come down to rest in the branches.

"And we had excellent company. Lady Selina was ever so charming in her quiet way. The most amazing thing about her kindness in always thinking of others first is that she never makes one uneasy with it. Most people who insist on putting others first merely call attention to themselves by the act."

Elizabeth kissed her sister-in-law good-night. "I'm pleased you had a pleasant evening, Dear." Mary nodded in reply.

"We breakfast at Spring Gardens in the morning. Will you go with us?"

Mary's peevishness almost made her refuse, but just in time her common sense prevailed and she accepted.

The next morning, clad in her most charming straw bonnet decorated with cherry ribbons and bobbin lace, and wearing a *levette*, a simple loose gown with a sash cut from silk of shaded pink and crimson stripes on a ground of pale cream, Mary rode in the carriage with her mother, Elizabeth, and Clement to the dock where their party was assembling to take the ferry to the Gardens on the other side of the River Avon.

In spite of her confused feelings about Rowland, she was determined that her smile should match the brightness of the morning. When they first met those from the Countess' party, Mary felt the barrier of Rowland's new coldness; but then the Countess, who had surprised everyone by accepting Elizabeth's invitation, prodded him between the shoulders with her walking stick. "Rowly, offer Miss Tudway your arm." And Mary could see his irrepressible humor conquer his reluctance.

"At your service, Miss Tudway." He extended his hand, Mary placed hers atop, and they stepped onto the gently rocking ferry boat behind Lady Selina, likewise holding Colonel Hasting's hand for support.

As Selina and her Colonel took seats in front of Mary and Rowland in the ferry, Mary considered her friends and the happy future in store for them. According to Elizabeth's report, Colonel George Hastings, two years Lady Selina's senior, had been brought up with her elder brother under the Earl's care at Donnington Park, their family seat, so that their present friendship was based on a lifetime of companionship.

As Francis, Earl of Huntingdon, had shown little inclination to marry, and as Colonel Hasting's elder brother was childless, the great possibility was that Colonel Hastings would succeed to the Earldom of Huntingdon, and that there would be another Selina, Countess of Huntingdon.

But what meant even more to Mary was the adoring gleam in the military man's eyes when he looked at Lady Selina, and the charming, almost shy manner in which she returned his regard; it seemed a glow of gentle happiness surrounded Selina. The blissful ending in store for the couple made Mary smile and reflect that it couldn't befall two nicer people.

As soon as they were midway across the river, they could hear the strains of French horns and clarinets playing in the Gardens. Spring Garden had been laid out as a charming retreat for visitors to Bath, with acres of walks and ponds and ornamental beds of flowers bordering the blue Avon.

The party made their way along the sweetly scented, hyacinth-bordered path to the long room where breakfast was served. The invigorating atmosphere of fresh air, sparkling scenery, and pleasant companions encouraged Mary to approach the meal of Spring Garden cakes and rolls and pots of chocolate with abandon. But the party at the next table was less circumspect than that got up by Elizabeth, and their laughter and gossip reached the ears of Mary and her companions. "And then Miss Braddock, enamored of such a complete rogue, spent six thousand pounds in paying his debts and lost both money and lover."

Lady Huntingdon's voice cut sharply across their story, undoubtedly reaching tables beyond her own. "And they think it a matter for levity. Rogues, charlatans, mountebanks, and strumpets—that's who lies behind the pomp and elegant facade of this city. Just like that folly of Mr. Allen's—Sham Castle, indeed! A great castle on a hill that's nothing but a front to look at. Fah! That's all these fribbles of society are—just outward show with no thought for their eternal souls.

"All about, one sees the vice, intrigue, and corruption of a society which values pleasure and luxury and nothing else—a jostling crowd of highborn and lowborn all engaged in a frantic round of pleasure and diversion. They should look to the healing of their souls rather than their bodies."

Elizabeth looked distinctly uncomfortable at this breakfast table homily. In her unobtrusive way, Lady Selina signaled a footman to offer one of the plainer buns to her mother. The diversion was successful for only a few moments, however, as Lady Huntingdon's determined chin rose and her snapping eyes and sharp words compelled the company to her attention. "But judgment will not always be stayed, as in the case of the young man who dropped dead after dancing thirty-three *couple* in the Assembly Rooms. His partner fainted, but was at it again after being revived by spirit of hartshorn and tincture of tiddlen. She had another chance; but his soul was required of him that very night, as it someday will be of us all."

It appeared for a moment that the lesson was at an end, but then the Countess' sharp eyes spotted a couple at a nearby table openly conducting an amatory dalliance. She sniffed loudly. "Men come here to be cured of the pox. But they are more like to bring it on than cure it." Having unburdened her soul, Her Ladyship at last turned her attention to her plate.

"Would you prefer tea, Mama? I'm persuaded your chocolate must be quite cold." Selina gave her mother a sweet smile and again signaled the footman.

"You are all my support and stay, Selina," the Countess said in an uncharacteristically soft voice, then turned to Elizabeth. "She is the only one left to me; my husband and other children are all dead except the young Earl who lives in London with Lord Chesterfield." With a look of tenderness which Mary would not have credited had she not seen it herself, the Countess' eyes filled with tears. Lady Selina again smiled at her mother and the conversation around the table became general.

By now, Mary was aware of a slight tightness of her sash and set her last cake aside unfinished, even though it had a filling containing her favorite almond paste.

Lady Selina, seated across from her, asked, "Would you care to take a turn through the parterre?"

"Indeed. I find formal gardens most charming," Mary quickly agreed.

71

The ever-attentive Colonel Hastings hurried to assist the ladies with their chairs and was fumbling to hand them their parasols when the Countess' voice rang sharply down the table, "Rowly!"

His slow grin lighted his eyes and he stepped to her chair. "You would care for a stroll, my Lady?"

"I would not. For the son of a Baronet, you are very slack in your duty to the young ladies."

Rowland bowed. "I thank Your Ladyship for reminding me of my duty." He extended his hand, palm downward, to Mary.

She took it in silence, but when they were out of hearing of the rest of the party, following several paces behind Selina and the Colonel, Mary said, "Rowly, why have you been avoiding me?"

"Ah, I would not like to damage your social position—a thing most easily accomplished in this gossip-ridden town—by having it voiced abroad that you have taken up with an enthusiast."

"Do not be absurd. I have heard that Mr. Wesley's sermons are very popular in town."

"Quite so. Above five thousand attended his first sermon here. But whether that is an indication of spiritual hunger or merely a desire for entertainment is uncertain. Wesley thought it unlikely the Gospel could have a place where Satan's throne is."

"Satan's throne?" Mary recalled the Countess' words at the breakfast table. "Surely that is an exaggeration."

"Perhaps. Wesley once said the people of Bath are all children of wrath and their natural tempers are corrupt and abominable. The sheriff asked him on his next visit not to preach; but he continued until the local authorities realized the benefit of his work for the moral ease and quiet of the place, and a member of the city corporation presented him with a roasted ox."

"And do you expect your own irregular preaching to have such a happy outcome?"

But Rowland would not be drawn to discussing his personal affairs. "Pray, what should I want with a roasted ox? But truth to tell, not all Wesley's confrontations achieved success. At the time when nothing occurred in Bath without the authority of the Master of Ceremonies, Beau Nash asked him by what authority he was preaching. Wesley replied, 'By that of Jesus Christ, conveyed to me by the present Archbishop of Canterbury, when he laid his hands upon me and said, "Take thou authority to preach the Gospel!" ' Nash, however, protested that it was contrary to law, adding, 'Besides, your preaching frightens people out of their wits.' 'Sir, did you ever hear me preach?' Wesley asked. The Beau replied that he had not. 'How then can you judge of what you have never heard?' 'By common report.' 'Sir, is not your name Nash? I dare not judge of the things I hear of you by common report!'

"Nash accepted the challenge to hear Mr. Wesley and later commented that it was no difficult matter for the Methodists to preach extempore, since they had a certain string of words and expressions that they consistently used on every subject. 'It is such a string as must draw you to heaven,' Wesley replied, 'if ever you intend to go there.' 'I thank you,' said Nash, 'but I don't choose to go to heaven on a string.' "

The story was told lightly as a diversion; but the fact that Beau Nash, who at that time had been the uncrowned king of Bath had now gone to his eternal reward, added an unspoken gravity. The Beau was no longer spending his time ruling the aristocracy, but was reaping the consequence of his choices. Mary walked quietly for some time, apparently lost in admiration of the bright spring flowers around the ponds; but she was really considering the story Rowland had told and the earlier words of the Countess, in contrast to the life she had been leading; and more immediately disturbing, Rowland's reticence to discuss his personal affairs. This was the same Rowland who had been her laughing companion on family occasions since childhood; and yet he was accompanying her now only at the direct order of the Countess, and with the formality of a newly introduced stranger. She had seen flickers of amusement warm his eyes briefly in the last two days, but not once had his affectionate smile rested on her. He had come yesterday specifically to report that his troubles at the University were settled quite satisfactorily. But it was obvious that he was worried about something.

Their rambling walk had taken them in a circular pattern and they were now approaching again the long room when two familiar male figures appeared on the path in front of them. Roger and Westmoreland made sweeping bows, and Westmoreland, who possessed an alarming memory for poetry, greeted them with a quotation from the *New Bath Guide* describing the Spring Garden breakfasts.

> " . . and there all went,
> On purpose to honor this great entertainment;
> The company made a most brilliant appearance,
> And ate bread and butter with great perseverance;
> All the chocolate too that my lord set before 'em,
> The ladies despatch'd with the utmost decorum,
> Soft musical numbers were heard all around,
> The horns' and the clarions' echoing sound."

"I trust you've had a pleasant breakfast, Miss Tudway." Roger again swept an arch with his pale blue tricorn, then fixed Rowland with a challenging stare. "But it grieves me to find one of such tender sensibilities as you in the company of a noted irreligious."

Rowland remained expressionless at the taunt in the guise of a witticism, but Mary flew to his defense. "Irreligious! I beg your pardon, Sir. Mr. Hill is exceeding religious! He's fanatical in it."

"Ah, exactly so." Roger smiled. "A regular fanatic—or is that irregular?"

Mary drew herself up taller. "Not so! His preaching may be irregular, but—"

At this point, Rowland, his lip quivering with amusement intervened. "Pray, Mary, cease defending me while I still have a shred of reputation left."

Again Roger bowed. "Forsooth, forgive me if I have offended. I had thought to compliment, but now I have quite lost track of the conversation."

"If you meant to say I am religious, I indeed take it as a compliment." Rowland's voice was mild.

"As would your friend, Lady Huntingdon, I believe. My uncle informs me there is to be a celebration at the Pope's—er, I mean, Her Ladyship's—chapel. I think I shall attend; it would be great fun to sit in the Nicodemus Chamber with Uncle."

Westmoreland, who always had a ready store of poetry, quoted,

> "Hearken, Lady Betty, hearken,
> to the dismal news I tell;
> How your friends are all embarking
> for the fiery gulph of Hell:
> Cards and dances ev'ry day,
> Jenny laughs at Tabernacle—"

74

Roger interrupted his friend with a stricken pose. "But I forget myself. Is there indeed to be a celebration? There is a rumor here, in everybody's mouth, that the Countess is confined, or has run in debt and squandered away a great deal more than her annuity upon vagabond preachers and places for them to preach in. I cannot learn with any certainty what the case really is; but there is something or another at the bottom of this rumor which will soon be better known."

Westmoreland picked up his story. "We are told that her son has taken out a statute of lunacy against her, that madness is incident to the family, and that she is sister to that Lord who was hanged at Tyburn not long since for willfully killing his man. And worse yet, a nephew of hers, Walter Shirley, has published a volume of Methodist sermons."

"No! Now, I say, Westmoreland, if you are to recount tales stricken in years, I much prefer the one of Beau Nash's vintage. After he had attended one of her drawing rooms in suitably somber attire, verses appeared pinned to the pillars of the Pump Room stating that the Countess, attended by a saintly sister, was to preach in that room the next morning; and that Mr. Nash, to be known henceforth as the Rev. Richard Nash, was expected to preach in the evening in the Assembly Room. It was hoped that the audience would be numerous, as a collection was intended for the Master of Ceremonies, retiring from office."

Mary, who would ordinarily have been diverted by these stories, now recalled the touch of genuine emotion she had witnessed on Her Ladyship's face and felt a quick, rising anger that such a lady, no matter how medievally autocratic, should be the butt of unkind jokes. "The Countess of Huntingdon is a fine and upright lady who serves God according to her own conscience, and I will thank you not to make light of her in my presence." She snapped her fan for emphasis and turned so sharply she almost slammed into Rowland. To her own amazement, hot, angry tears stung her eyes.

As Mary and Rowland rejoined their party, and all the way on the ferry back across the river, and then in the carriage to the Royal Crescent, Mary didn't say a word. She couldn't understand what was wrong with her. Bath had proved to be everything she had dreamed of and more; she had attended more balls, more concerts, and more parties in a month here than she had thought to enjoy in a lifetime; and she had a beau of the first fashion who was, if anything, overattentive.

What more did she want? And why was she worried about Rowland? He would take his degree, and then it was but a short step to the ordination he had his heart set on. And his cooled demeanor toward her seemed to make it clear that she needn't worry any longer about his making her a troublesome offer. So why didn't that cheer her?

Instead of turning into their own doorway with Elizabeth, Mary said she thought she would just step down the way and have a chat with Sarah.

The girls settled comfortably in Sarah's blue-and-white bedroom, and Mary inadvertently set the tone for the conversation by letting a depressed sigh escape her. "Sarah, do you ever feel empty?" Sarah's startled look showed she had no idea what her friend was getting at. "That is, do you ever get tired of the routine?"

Sarah's infectious laugher filled the room. "Mary, what nonsense you do talk! Tired of having fun, of being admired by beaux, of buying pretty fripperies? Are you chaffing me? That's not possible. You don't mean to say *you* are weary of it, do you?"

Mary sighed again.

"Goodness, you are moped! You need a rest, that's all. You aren't tired of having fun; you're just plain tired, that's all. Go home now for a nice lie-down and then we'll find a new diversion—or at least a new bonnet to purchase."

Sarah had made it clear. Whatever was bothering her, the problem was with herself; her feelings were unnatural. Mary decided to let the matter drop.

But Sarah persevered. "And what of this Mr. Hill, Mary? I think too much time in his company has turned you melancholy, probably from boredom. I'll grant he is a Baronet's son and exceedingly handsome with excellent manners; but surely you wouldn't consider forming an attachment to a Methodist? Westmoreland assures me Roger is perfectly taken with you—and he is his uncle's heir. Now *there's* a catch worth setting your cap at."

"Sarah! What a vulgar expression. I haven't 'set my cap' at anyone and have no intention of doing so. I simply find myself a bit fatigued, as you say. At any rate, a Baronet's son becoming a Methodist may be an oddity, but he's certainly not a bore."

"And Roger is?" Sarah asked in shocked tones.

"Well, he's very amusing, but that's all. There seems to be no real depth to him. I don't believe he ever really thinks about anything of importance."

Sarah obviously could not believe her ears. "Importance! He knows all the latest fashion and has an endless flow of entertaining gossip, and I heard him reading some charming poetry to you the other day. What more could you want?"

Mary didn't know. But as she walked slowly back to Number Six, attended by Sarah's abigail, she thought over her own words. Rowland Hill could be irritating, maddening, and worrisome, but he was never boring. She laughed quite as much in his company as she did in Roger's; but Rowland's companionship had the added quality of making her think, even if the thoughts weren't always comfortable.

· *6* ·

BACK AT THE VINEYARDS, the Countess of Huntingdon's house in Harlequin Row, Rowland was engaged in his own soul-searching about his intentions toward Mary. Had it not been for Berridge's warning, he would be the happiest of men, feeling assured of his future and basking in the company of the woman he adored. Or, if the Master of John's had refused him, he could have taken comfort from Berridge, assuming all would be for the best if he were to remain a lay itinerant, a life which—even if he was the son of a Baronet—he could in no wise ask a woman to share.

But as matters stood, to be with Mary when he felt he must resist her, and believed he had no right to challenge Roger's attentions for a place in her heart, produced despairing agony which his normally cheerful outlook left him unequipped to handle.

Perhaps he had misunderstood his old mentor's advice. He felt a sudden longing for the venerable man to be there that they might discuss his admonitions more fully. Rowland went in search of Her Ladyship, hoping she might have received word that Berridge was to attend the anniversary. He found her in her upstairs parlor, glowering out of one of the gothic windows which lined the front of the building.

"I can't think what they were about, making those Paragon Buildings seven stories high. One would think they set out to scrape the sky. It's a wonder God didn't strike them down as at the Tower of Babel. Formerly we had a quite perfect view from these windows." She turned to look at Rowland. "And what may I do for you, Sir?"

"I have come to inquire if you have received word from Berridge, Your Ladyship. Will he attend the anniversary?"

"I have, and he will not." She crossed the room with quick, measured steps, picked up a letter from her desk, and read,

"As for myself, I am now determined not to quit my charge. Never do I leave my bees though for a short space only, but at my return I find them either casting a colony or fighting and robbing each other; not gathering honey from every flower in God's garden, but filling the air with their buzzing, and darting out the venom of their little hearts in their fiery stings. Nay, so inflamed they often are, and a mighty little thing disturbs them, that three months' tinkering afterwards with a warming pan will scarce hive them at last and make them settle to work again."

Rowland, whose smile had grown throughout the reading, chuckled at the closing illusion.

"I suppose you find this amusing, do you? You and Berridge share the same besetting sin. Humor, Sir, is most inappropriate and unbecoming in a man of God. You must work to expunge it from your nature."

Rowland considered inquiring why she thought God had made him so if He had no use for the commodity; but not feeling equal to a lecture on original sin at the moment, he merely bowed as his answer.

The anniversary service celebrating the seventh year of the opening of the Countess of Huntingdon's Bath Chapel was to be held at six o'clock in the evening on the Sunday following Easter. Mrs. Child had declined the invitation, but the entire Tudway party was to attend. Mary chose a small but lavishly trimmed hat and set it at a sharp angle on her elaborately dressed hair, highly pleased with the new style Bath's most fashionable hairdresser had created for her. She picked up a wide, black silk scarf edged with frills and allowed Elizabeth's dresser to drape it carefully around her shoulders just before Mrs. Tudway knocked at her door. "Are you ready, my Dear?"

"Coming, Mother." Mary turned toward the door. "Oh, I almost forgot my ticket." She moved the numerous pots and jars around on her dressing table until she uncovered the small strip of cardboard. "Other Foundation can no man lay, than that is laid, which is Jesus Christ. 1 Corinthians 3:11." She read the text to her mother.

"Yes, my Dear, but no matter what it says, I do believe Her Ladyship has laid quite a few foundation stones. I understand she has built something like fifteen chapels and staffed them with chaplains at her own expense—at Brighton, Tunbridge, Wells, Dover, in Wales and Derbyshire. It makes one quite tired to think of such energy." Mrs. Tudway led the way to their carriage.

Mary was mildly surprised to meet Roger just outside the door to the chapel, but she was completely amazed that Bishop Twysden should be there too. She presented her family to the important guest, then remained with Roger as the others went in. "How gracious of you to attend the Countess' celebration, Bishop Twysden," Mary said. "I'm sure Her Ladyship will be sensible of the honor you do her."

The Bishop laughed and held out his ringed hand for Mary to curtsy over, his lawn sleeves billowing over his wrist. "I doubt she will feel honored; more likely, invigorated by the opportunity to convert me."

"Convert you?" Mary was astounded.

"Oh, yes. Her Ladyship is convinced of the sinfulness of all men, no matter of what station."

"But, that's impossible—a Bishop. Surely you were baptized—"

"In my infancy, at Westminster Abbey, with a Bishop presiding, and later confirmed. But what is good enough for the church isn't necessarily good enough for the Countess." Rather than leading the way through the main door, the Bishop walked farther toward the back of the building to a small door. "The Countess was most thoughtful in her accommodations, however. Realizing that higher members of the church might feel—ah—uncomfortable among her more enthusiastic worshipers, she has provided us with a private chamber. Would you care to see?"

The Bishop opened the door on a small room to the right of the pulpit, curtained from the general view. The cubicle contained a comfortable padded chair, a tiny fireplace, and a special niche where the Bishop could set his claret. Here he could see the service only imperfectly through a tiny window, but he could hear clearly, without the disgrace of being seen in such a place.

"Perfectly cozy, is it not? I understand even the Archbishop of

Dublin has occupied this eccentric Bishop's Seat." Bishop Twysden arranged his robes carefully in the chair, poured out a glass of claret and set it at hand in the niche. "Yes, I believe this will do quite well to view what Horace Walpole termed, 'Mr. Wesley's opera.' " He took a long sip of claret, then waved his hand. "Run along now, Children. This should prove most amusing."

Mary and Roger found seats near her family; but unlike the comforts provided for the Bishop, they were obliged to sit upon forms—long, backless benches. Even the galleries behind and on both sides of them were full; it was clear that Lady Huntingdon's celebration was to be one of the events of the season.

"Most appropriate that this should have been built in Harlequin Row," Roger observed. "We shall no doubt be treated to comic entertainment. What do you suppose those eagles signify?" He waved a scented, lace-edged handkerchief in the direction of three large, white, spread-winged eagles that stood behind the ornamental iron altar rail.

"They are very handsome, aren't they?" Mary replied. "Perhaps they are from the Huntingdon family crest? At any rate, they make most unusual reading desks."

The preacher's eagle was in the center of a platform, elevated three steps higher than the others with a heavy, dark oak pulpit behind it. Behind the other eagles were scarlet damask chairs. It was very striking in the high, white room. But Mary was most taken with the elaborate candelabra. On each side of the pulpit were eight branches with five candles in each branch, and so on around the room, until there must have been upwards of a hundred candles lighting the chapel.

Roger, who had also been looking around, tugged at the lace frill on his sleeve and said, "Faith, I am glad to see that luxury is creeping upon them before persecution."

Mary was spared making an answer to this as the organ pealed an anthem from the gallery behind them, signaling the start of the service. The Countess and her entourage of fine ladies with a few male escorts took their places in chairs down front, and the officiating clergymen walked to the scarlet seats behind their eagles. Mary caught her breath when she saw that Rowland was in the reader's seat on her left. She had no idea that among the many notable visitors, he would be chosen for so important a post.

She had a vague feeling she should recognize the fine-featured man with the luminous brown eyes and finely curled white hair in the preacher's seat, who stood to lead the congregation in singing,

> Jesus, Lover of My soul,
> Let me to Thy bosom fly.
> While the nearer waters roll,
> While the tempest still is high!
> Hide me, O my Saviour, Hide,
> Till the storm of life is past.
> Safe into the haven guide,
> Oh, receive my soul at last!

Mary then recognized him as the composer of the hymn, Charles Wesley. She was interested in seeing and hearing him because of the fame of his singing and preaching, and of the work of his more renouned brother, John, in starting the Methodist Society. But the honored guest became even more intriguing to her when a lady who was introduced as his wife joined him and together they sang, "Love Divine, All Loves Excelling." It was clear that they were singing of God's love, which they had experienced personally; but it also seemed to Mary that when the song spoke of "Joy of heav'n to earth come down," their expressions took on a double meaning, as if they had also experienced an earthly love with each other for which they praised their God.

Sally Wesley had a fine figure in a modestly cut round gown of a heavy blue fabric. The white lawn fischu filling in the square-cut neckline highlighted her bright eyes and sweet smile; but Mary was shocked at the heavily pockmarked skin which quite spoiled her looks. She must have been beautiful before she was stricken with the smallpox, Mary thought. What a pity!

Whatever the illness had done to the lady's appearance, however, it had done nothing to mar the beauty of her voice.

> Finish then Thy new creation;
> Pure and spotless let us be.
> Let us see Thy great salvation,
> Perfectly restored in Thee.
> Changed from glory into glory
> Till in heav'n we take our place.
> Till we cast our crowns before Thee,
> Lost in wonder, love and praise.

And at the end of the song, Sally Wesley's first smile was for her husband; then for the congregation.

Rowland stood to read the lesson for the day, from 1 John 5, " 'Whatsoever is born of God overcometh the world; and this is the victory that overcometh the world, even our faith.' " Mary, who was perfectly acquainted with his conversational voice, had never heard Rowland address an audience, and was held spellbound at the extraordinary clarity and sweetness of his words as he continued the passage. And she was amazed at the elegance of his appearance as he stood behind the large white eagle in a plain black suit. Not yet ordained, he was not wearing clerical garments as the other clergymen on the platform; she could never have guessed that a man could look so handsome in drab black with no lace, embroidery, or metallic trim.

" 'And this is the record, that God hath given to us eternal life; and this life is in His Son. He that hath the Son hath life; and he that hath not the Son hath not life.' "

Mary felt bereft when he quit reading—she could have listened to him for hours. But the lesson was followed by a choir of boys and girls who sang hymns to Scottish ballad tunes. When they began their third melody, Roger leaned close to her and commented in a not entirely hushed voice, "They have charming voices, but they sing so long one would think they were already in eternity and knew how much time they had before them."

Mary gave him a disapproving look which silenced his cynical humor, and at last the children finished their songs. The clergyman sitting behind the eagle on the right, whose outstanding features were his gentle smile and long, lank hair, rose and led the congregation in prayer—not simply reading the collect from the prayer book, "Almighty Father, who hast given thine only Son to die for our sins, and to rise again for our justification," but continuing on *in his own words* at the end of the printed prayer, his soft Swiss dialect giving the words a special emphasis. Mary had never heard such a thing and was shocked into lifting her head and looking around her. She found that many of the most fashionably dressed worshipers had a similar reaction, and an undertone of astonished whispers accompanied the prayer.

Then Charles Wesley mounted the steps to the center eagle and read his text. "There was a man of the Pharisees, named Nicodemus, a ruler of the Jews. The same came to Jesus by night." As the reading continued, Mary smiled, wondering what the Bishop, tucked away in his Nicodemus Chamber, thought of the text. " 'Verily, verily I say unto thee, Except a man be born again, he cannot see the kingdom of God.' "

The preacher paused, surveyed his audience, then spoke with a level voice that reached to the farthest corners of the galleries. "The greatest sham of our age is the same as in Nicodemus' age—the profession of religion without knowing its power. The hypocrisy which hides the hideous deformity of a Christless character by the cloak of a plausible profession is one of the most odious of which a man is capable."

Wesley smiled at Lady Huntingdon sitting before him. "We are gathered here today to celebrate a great occasion in the work of the Kingdom—the opening of this chapel in one of the most wicked cities of our nation. If ever my mind felt the solemn weight of those words of the good Patriarch Jacob, 'Surely this is none other but the house of God and the gate of heaven,' it is on this present occasion. Can we suppose that so many of God's ministers and people should find it in their hearts to assemble together on such a glorious design, and He not be present with them? Oh, surely not! We believe Him to be in the midst of us. Nor can anything short of His special preference crown our labors with success. What a mercy then, that we live in a day in which the Lord's promise is, we hope, to be remarkably verified, 'Behold, I am with you alway, even unto the end of the world.'

"Matters of salvation are of infinite importance. The glory of bringing souls to Christ is the greatest honor God can confer upon us. The salvation of one soul is of more worth than a thousand worlds. My dearest brothers and sisters, may God fill us with like ardent desires to those which warmed the apostle's heart, when he was constrained to declare to his Galatian hearers, that he travailed in birth till Christ was formed in them.

"And in this mighty congregation, if there are those here—and I am persuaded there are—who do not know this divine power and assurance in their own life, let me proclaim to you that this divine happiness and peace is unto all men and women."

The preacher's words caught at Mary's heart. Could the ennui she had been feeling indicate a spiritual need? She cast back in her mind to her feelings of boredom in Wells, which she had attributed to the need for more social excitement. Had she looked for her solution in entirely the wrong place?

But how could her need be spiritual? She was baptized. As her thoughts groped for assurance, she turned the pages of her prayer book to the Baptism of Infants. "Dearly beloved, forasmuch as all men are conceived and born in sin; and that our Saviour Christ saith, 'None can enter into the kingdom of God, except he be regenerate and born anew of water and of the Holy Ghost' . . . ye have brought this child here to be baptized, ye have prayed that our Lord Jesus Christ would vouchsafe to receive him, to release him of his sins, to sanctify him with the Holy Ghost, to give him the kingdom of heaven, and everlasting life. . . . Our Lord Jesus Christ has promised in His gospel to grant·all these things that ye have prayed for. . . . This infant must promise by you that are his sureties, *until he come of age to take it upon himself,* that he will renounce the devil and all his works, and constantly believe God's holy word and obediently keep His commandments."

Well, she supposed she had taken the promise upon herself. She attended divine service regularly and fully believed all the creeds.

Certainly she shared none of Rowland's enthusiasm which could lead one into socially unacceptable extremes, but she was not a heathen. She did believe. She could see no solution for her problem in seeking spiritual fervor, but she determined to talk to Rowland about the matter.

The service concluded with another extempore prayer by the kind-looking minister with the lank hair, who was identified as John Fletcher. Then Mary's thoughts were lost in a bustle of gathering her parasol, prayer book, and scarf. "I must confess, the lessons were read very well and the hymns sung very sweetly," Roger announced. "Had there been no preaching, which was in the highest attitude of rhapsody and rant, nor extempore prayer, the whole would have been much to my satisfaction. I found the old praying parson to be a perfect specimen—he has true Methodistical hair."

Elizabeth made her way to Mary through the press. "We are to attend a private reception in the Countess' rooms. Will you come with us?"

Mary glanced uncertainly at Roger. "Egad! Such stamina. I beg I may be excused. I feel quite surfeited with holiness." And then in a voice which only Mary could hear, "And I have no doubt my poor uncle will be entirely overcome. If the first improvised prayer

85

didn't knock him up completely, I'm persuaded the second one may have finished the poor fellow off. He will be in want of my support to see him home to something stronger than that claret he was fortified with." And making a sweeping bow, Roger left.

Mary was happy to join her family in the elegant drawing room next to the chapel. Having the Countess' living quarters attached to the chapel meant that it was constituted by law a private chapel, and that Her Ladyship had complete authority over its services and ministers.

Mary would have liked to congratulate Rowland upon his fine reading, but he was surrounded by a group of important-looking clergymen and ladies of the Countess' private party; so she went instead to the long table bearing an elegant cold collation. She took a generous portion of orange souffle and was helping herself to the celerata cream when Lady Selina joined her. "Don't miss the ratafia biscuits; they're my favorite." She pointed to a footed plate just beyond the pastry basket. "Did you enjoy the service? I thought the children's choir charming."

Mary agreed. "And the Wesleys were—" she faltered for the right word. She had meant to say enchanting, but that seemed too frivolous for music so profound.

"Quite sublime, are they not?" Selina finished for her. "Would you like me to present you to Sally? She's one of the people I most admire in the entire world—an opinion shared by all who know her, but especially by her husband."

"Yes, I could tell, just seeing them together. I was most taken by the radiance of it. She is so beautiful in spite of—"

"The smallpox? Yes, they had been married just five years when Sally's sister Becky, who was living with them, was inoculated. She brought the illness home with her. Their tiny son, Jacky, died of it, and for weeks Charles despaired of saving Sally. But when the fever was spent and she was left as you see her now, Charles declared he loved her more than ever—this disease removed the one barrier to the perfection of their union. You see, Sally is twenty years younger than her husband, but now they look the same age. And she thanked God she had chosen not to be inoculated."

Mary shook her head in silent awe of a love that could be so self-sacrificing, so unhindered by outward appearance. Just then Colonel Hastings joined them, tall and handsome in his regimentals; and when Mary saw the smile that passed between him and Selina,

86

she felt sure another such match was in the making. "Yes, I should be most honored to be presented to Mrs. Wesley," Mary said.

Sally Wesley was as gracious in person as she had appeared on the platform. She made Mary welcome to their circle, then went on telling the Countess of their two musically gifted sons, whom Charles felt would far outshine their father in the world of composing and performing; and of their six-year-old daughter, Selina, named for the Countess of Huntingdon.

And across the room, Rowland, with such concerns much on his mind of late, had also noted the special bond between Charles Wesley and his wife, and had separated the preacher from the others to question him of Berridge's tenets regarding marriage.

"It may be so for some," Charles Wesley spoke thoughtfully. "Certainly, if Berridge feels it would be wrong for him to marry, then it would be—God leads us each according to His Holy will. I can speak only for myself. God gave Sally to me to love. And she has been of inestimable value to my work."

"To your work?"

"Indeed. My brother John for a time shared Berridge's views and was opposed to our attachment on that grounds. But he came about and finally married us himself."

"And there was truly no cause for his concern? I beg your forgiveness if I seem to pry, but I have wrestled much with this lately."

"A very valid question for any young man. Certainly, marriage changed the nature of my work. I have undoubtedly done more hymn-writing with Sally's fine musicianship to help me, and my ministry has been in a more settled area around Bristol. Not many family men can put in thousands of miles of circuit riding in a year. But who is to say one is of more value to the kingdom than the other? And the slack left by one man is always taken up by another." He looked up to smile at the other man who had shared the pulpit with them that evening. "And our dear Fletcher is another case in point." He gave the name its Swiss pronunciation, Flechaire. "His beloved wife was taken from him at an early age, but she worked with him heart and soul during the short time their union lasted. She was of enormous service to his presidency of Lady Huntingdon's College at Trevecca and made their vicarage at Madeley a haven for all who came to them weary and heavy-laden, sick and sorrowful."

Others joined them and the conversation became general; but Rowland could not rid his mind of Wesley's phrase as he looked across the room at his beautiful sister-in-law, "God gave her to me to love."

The next day, while not on the Bath social calendar as the Countess' celebration had been, was an exciting one for the Tudway family. Mr. Tudway was to arrive about noon and the family was to go together to Thomas Gainsborough's house, at Number Seventeen the Royal Circus, to see the finished portraits. Now that the work was completed, Mrs. Tudway was filled with anxiety. What if her husband was not pleased with the outcome of her project? What if he still refused to have his portrait painted and her picture would hang alone in the dining room? Had she been wrong to choose her emerald green gown to be painted in? Perhaps the amber would have been more becoming? Was it a mistake to pose in her white lace calash? Perhaps a smaller cap with lappets would have been more flattering?

Rowland joined the family to see his sister's portrait; as it was a fine day, the entire party chose to walk the short distance down Brock Street to the studio.

The painter met them at the door of his home, clad in teal velvet coat and breeches, with a red waistcoat, his rich brown hair tied at the nape of his neck. His clear eyes shown with pleasure as he led the way to his painting room. "I am so happy you could join us today, Mr. Tudway. I believe you will be most pleased with your wife's portrait—and those of your son and daughter-in-law as well." His arm swept an arc around the room, as if he were presenting the company to the portraits, rather than the other way around.

Mary was the first to speak. "O Mama, you look perfectly lovely! Exactly the sensible, competent creature you are. And how clever of you to choose your green gown; it just sets off your eyes." Hannah visibly relaxed under her daughter's approval.

"And your choice of cap," Rowland added. "It shines like a halo against the dark background."

When her husband agreed, Mrs. Tudway could have been no closer to heaven. "Fine work he made of you too, Clement." Squire Tudway stood before the head-and-shoulders portrait of his aquiline-featured son in a red coat with brass buttons, his powdered hair curled just above his ears. "Very fine, just the right dignity for a member of Parliament."

He continued on around the room to the easel bearing the waist-length portrait of Elizabeth. "Well, Hill, did you know your sister to be such a beauty? Very fine, very fine." He turned to the artist. "I congratulate you, Sir."

"O Elizabeth, it's perfect," Mary said. "You couldn't have chosen a lovelier ornament than the pearls in your hair and at your neck and at the yoke of your dress."

Elizabeth laughed. "I'm glad you approve, Mary, but it was Mr. Gainsborough who selected the pearls. The rose dress was my selection."

Gainsborough rang for refreshments and soon his housekeeper was handing round wine and biscuits while the family continued to discuss the details of the portraits. "Papa, you must be painted full-length like Mama," Mary said abruptly, and with that note of decision in her voice that her family knew all too well. "Perhaps out-of-doors," she continued. "As Mama is sitting by an open window, it would be a charming idea to think that you are in her view."

Charles Tudway considered for a moment, while Hannah held her breath. "In my brown frock coat, do you think, Daughter?" His smile spoke his consent.

The rest of the family was to return to the Crescent to dine, but Mary had hoped to do some shopping that afternoon. Maria had informed them that, indeed, the wonderful event Mrs. Tudway had hoped for would occur in the summer, and Mary thought this an excellent excuse to visit the toymaker's shop in Milsom Street. "May I accompany you?" Rowland asked. "Or would you prefer your maid to go with you?"

Mary returned his smile, "Indeed, Sir, as you are much stronger than Minson, you will do much better as a package-bearer." Mary was surprised by the warmth she felt return to Rowland's attitude toward her. She was still mystified as to the cause of his earlier aloofness, but found herself more pleased than she could have imagined at its passing. The toyman presented a delightful assortment of cleverly carved toys and beautifully dressed dolls, tiny china tea sets, and bags of shiny marbles. After careful consideration, she chose a small carved bear with jointed legs on a stick.

That errand completed, Mary and Rowland both seemed hesitant whether to turn their steps back to the Crescent, or continue on downhill toward town. "Would you care to stop at Mr. Gill's for a jelly tart or a basin of vermicelli?" Rowland sugggested, as the pastry shop was only two doors down from them.

Mary considered. "I would like something, but perhaps not vermicelli right now. Are you acquainted with any tearooms?" They were quite near a coffeehouse, but that den of masculine gossip and politics was not a place to which a gentleman could escort a lady.

"Why, yes. Just on the other side of Abbey Green is Sally Lunn's House. We could take refreshment there."

They proceeded at a leisurely pace, admiring the goods arranged in the various shop windows to tempt the casual shopper. At a jeweler's they halted to take a closer look at his merchandise. Jeweled fans, hair ornaments, and gold snuffboxes took their places among the necklaces, brooches, and earrings. But one item caught Mary's eye. "O Rowly, look at those silver filagree shoe buckles! Have you ever seen finer workmanship? They have been made by a true artist." The delicate openwork buckles were ornamented with silver-petaled roses with a setting of pink jade in the center of each flower. Mary gazed at them for a full minute, then turned away.

"Let us go on. I am getting hungry," she said.

They had taken no more than six steps in their intended direction, however, when the door of the milliner's shop they were passing flew open and Sarah dashed out. "Mary, just the person I most wanted to see! You must come in at once. Mama and I are having a dreadful row over the suitability of this most charming hat with blue lace bows and lavender ostrich feathers. Do tell her it's not at all too old for me."

Mary was drawn into the shop by her friend, but Rowland asked to be excused, saying he would rejoin them in a moment. The contretemp was quickly settled by Mary pointing out another hat, lavishly trimmed with pink silk roses. "Oh, thank you, Mary. I knew I could rely on you. Look, Mama, the roses just match the embroidery on my new silk petticoat, do they not?" Sarah turned this way and that, so all could admire the hat perched atop her coiffure.

At that moment Rowland returned, and he and Mary resumed their progress. They were destined to be interrupted again, however, for as they neared the Abbey, a small dog ran out into the street in front of them, then sat in the gutter looking forlorn. "Oh, poor creature," Mary cried. "Do you suppose it's a spit dog?" The back alleys of Bath abounded with scraggly dogs which spent most of their lives running in metal wheels attached to geared machinery turning the spits roasting sides of beef in the huge fireplaces of the kitchens serving Bath's well-fed patrons.

"Indeed, I expect it is."

"Can't we do something for it, Rowly?"

"Shall I see if he'll come to me? We could at least treat him to a meaty bone that he didn't have to cook himself." Unconcerned about his coattails, Rowland knelt down on the cobbles and held out his hand. "Here, fella, come on, boy."

At the sound of a kind voice, the mutt perked up his ears. "Come on, this lady wants to be your friend." The dog took a step closer "Atta boy." Rowland scratched the little brown-and-white ears, then scooped the dog into his arms. "What shall we call him?"

Mary considered for a moment. "Spit. What else?"

Rowland laughed and scratched the dog again. "Spit, it is."

Then Mary took the small bundle of matted hair into her arms. "What a horrid practice, putting such sweet animals in wheels!"

"It is. But it's much harder making small boys sit by the fire and turn the crank for hours on end."

"Is there no alternative?"

Rowland considered for a moment. "Perhaps a system of weights attached to a wheel, something like a hall clock."

"Excellent! If I am ever mistress of a large kitchen, I shall require such a contrivance for the roasting."

Spit snuggled comfortably in Mary's arms and went to sleep. Just a step down off North Parade brought them to the Abbey Green and a small house with a bow-fronted window. The hostess at the door frowned at the blissfully dreaming Spit.

"The lady's particular pet," Rowland explained, as he removed his tricorn. The hostess showed them to a table in the window. No one would question the right of a lady of quality to take her lapdog with her wherever she chose—even if it was a scruffy specimen.

Rowland requested the waitress to bring coffee and a Sally Lunn apiece. A moment later, Mary gasped at the size of the Bath bun placed before her. "That's not a bun—it's an entire loaf!"

"Don't worry," her companion assured her. "It's all cloud."

One bite proved it to be the lightest bread one could imagine. They began making jokes about the difficulty of baking buns that insisted on rising and floating about the oven, and the possibility of Sally Lunn herself having been an angel to produce such airy fluff from flour and yeast.

It seemed to Mary that she had never known time to pass so swiftly or so pleasantly. But then the happy haze dissolved as reality intruded. "So now that the portraits are finished, you'll be leaving Bath?" Rowland asked.

Mary nodded, not willing to admit how little she looked forward to the departure—especially now that Rowland had come.

"Has it been a profitable time for you, Mary?"

Not for the world would she admit that the revels she so longed for had been the least bit of a letdown. "It has been exceedingly diverting," she said with forced enthusiasm.

Rowland regarded her levelly. "Mary, you needn't pretend with me. I don't know what's wrong. But I do know something has happened to put you in a pother, which you are trying very hard to bottle up."

"Oh, dear. Is it so obvious?"

"To me, yes, though I doubt anyone else would have noticed. I wish you would tell me what has destroyed your tranquillity." He paused. "But if you don't choose to, I won't press you."

She stroked the soft head of Spit curled drowsily in her lap. "I have become a bit wearied with all the gaity. Sarah says I need a rest and I expect she's right. But the thought of returning home to an endless round of neighborhood calls and *needlework*—" she gave a small shudder— "is not invigorating."

His long solemn look made her catch her breath. It was as if his eyes spoke words his mouth would not—words he was not ready to say, nor she to hear. If the moment had held and gone no further, it would have been perfect. But Rowland had a way of looking beyond her mind and heart to her very soul. And when his gaze seemed to touch a sore spot, her defenses came up.

"And have you no deeper need you wish to speak of, Mary? I am your friend. I would do anything in my power to help you."

"La, and what 'deeper need' could that be, Sir?" She unfolded her fan and fluttered it at him.

"I was thinking of spiritual matters, Mary." His voice was so soft that for an instant she thought she had imagined the words.

Then her temper flared. Was he accusing her of being an infi-
del? "Pray, and do you imagine yourself a priest that I should
confess to you? I was baptized as an infant and have attended
church all my life. My soul is quite the property of myself and the
church—not of an enthusiastic divinity student, I thank you, Sir."
She snapped her fan shut.

"No, Mary. One's soul is not the property of any person or
institution—even the church. It belongs to God, just as one's commitment must be to God. The church's rituals are merely dead
formality and will lead to death of the soul, if relied upon for
salvation."

"La, tell that to the mobs you preach to in the fields, Sir. Sally
Lunn's House is not the place for your irregular preaching. When I
want advice for my soul, I'll ask a Bishop—not your female pope."

Rowland's smile only fed her anger, "Ah yes, the Countess is
often called Her Holiness behind her back; but for all her dogmatic
ways you'd do better to listen to her than to your Bishop of
Raphoe."

"Rowland! How dare you abuse a Bishop? Have your
Methodistical manners made you lost to all sense of propriety? The
Bishop is a fine gentleman of elegance and learning and fashion
and—"

"And refinement," Rowland finished for her. "May I never be
the retailer of a whipt-syllabub divinity. Better to keep a cookshop
to satisfy the craving appetite than a confectioner's shop to regain
the depraved appetite of the dainty. Good brown-bread preaching
is best after all."

"A whipt-syllabub religion! Sir, is that what you would call the
established church? Why, I—"

In her agitation she leaned forward and knocked Spit's head
against the table, causing him to give a sharp yap which rang
through the small room.

Mary instantly leaned back in her chair and took refuge behind
her fan until the murmur of voices in the room resumed. But the
moment was all that was needed to cool the argument.

"Mary, I am to leave on the next morning but one. Tomorrow,
if your mother permits, will you accompany me to Wotton-under-
edge? I am to preach there, and you may see and judge for yourself
that which you argue against."

Mary agreed to the plan and Mrs. Tudway gave her permission;

so the next day Rowland and Mary drove northward out of Bath almost to the border of Wales. As it was to be a long drive, they left early and made such good time that they arrived ahead of the appointed hour for the service. Rowland drove on through the town and turned toward the Severn River. "Let me show you what I believe to be the most paradisiacal spot I have ever seen. I would that someday I might live here—or that heaven might be like this."

He stopped the carriage opposite a hillside which formed a perfect amphitheatre, three sides clothed with a wood, the other side open to a richly fertile dale. Rowland offered his hand and they walked to the top of the hill where Mary caught her breath at the landscape before her. As she turned slowly in all directions, the panorama changed from the Welsh mountains, the Malvern Hills, the rich vale of Berkley, to the broad course of the silvery and majestic Severn River. And in the foreground, grassy knolls and hanging woods blended in a scene of unspeakably lovely harmony. Before them was a rocky path winding through a sloping wood of beech; they followed it to an orchard where branches of bursting buds promised frostings of pink-and-white flowers, to be followed by succulent fruit.

Rowland looked at the trees for a moment. "I love to see the flowers and fruit which God makes the earth bring forth to please us, and then I think, oh, that I could bear more of the fruit of righteousness to please Him."

Mary was impressed by the solemnity of his thoughts, but displeased that in this romantic spot his words should be so pious. "O Rowly, is that all you think of—pleasing God?"

Rowland turned sharply to her and took her hand. "No, my dear Mary, there is another I would please too. If only it pleased her to be pleased by me."

"In faith, Sir, I can't follow all your pleases. But I'm sure it was a very pretty speech."

Mary found her heart was beating rapidly and she would have liked to continue that dialogue. But there was not time for more pretty speeches; for on the road below them they could see people coming up from the dales around, walking toward town to attend the promised preaching service. When they arrived at the marketplace, a great crowd had gathered. Rowland stood on a wagon in the center of the square and read his text from Ephesians 5:19,

"Awake, thou that sleepest—"

"Ann, that's the Baronet's son who goes about preaching," an old lady next to Mary said to another.

"Are you sure it's the Baronet's son himself?"

"Yes, that I am, for I saw his brother, Mr. Richard Hill, not long ago, and he is so like him, I am sure he is of the same family."

The women settled down to listen, but a man on Mary's other side seized a stone and pulled back his arm, taking careful aim at the preacher. Mary had a fleeting thought of flinging herself in front of the man when a burly arm reached from behind, grasped the arm holding the rock, and said in broad Gloucestershire dialect, "If thee dost touch him, I'll knock thy head off." The assailant dropped the stone and the people all became quiet, awed by the solemnity of the subject and the earnestness of the preacher. And Mary listened with particular closeness, hoping to find answers for some of the questions that had plagued her of late.

"Think particularly," the preacher urged his listeners, "whether you're choosing for time only, or for eternity. For, of course, a sensible person will wish to choose that which will be best on the long run. It is just as much part of the consideration what will be best for me between my thousandth and two-thousandth year as between my twentieth and thirtieth. It is curious how our estimate of time is altered by its being removed to a distance. Ask how long did Moses live before Christ. If a man says thirteen hundred years, and you correct him that it was fifteen hundred, he will reply, 'Pooh, why be so accurate? Within two hundred years will do.' But how immense two hundred years now seem!

"And so my friends, be certain that the choices you make are those that will last for eternity—choose to spend your life on those things that will count for as much two thousand years from now as twenty years from now, or twenty days from now."

Mary was thoughtful on the long drive back to Bath. There had been a power and a logic to Rowland's words that she couldn't deny; and yet she did not want to discuss them, for fear that bringing her thoughts into the open would force upon her a choice she was not yet ready to make.

"You are weary, Mary?" Rowland asked as they neared Bath. "You have not told me what you thought of the service."

"In faith, I'm not sure what I thought. I should have been outraged at such unseemly worship. And yet, there was a truth to the preacher's words." And that was as far as she would say.

When they reached the Royal Crescent, Rowland reached under the carriage seat and produced a small white package tied with red ribbons. "I leave Bath tomorrow, as you do. Think of me kindly as I prepare to take my degree and apply for ordination." He held the package to her.

She fumbled with the ribbons in her eagerness to see what Rowland could be giving her. How amazing that he should have thought to bring her a farewell gift. The paper fell away and Mary gasped with delight. A pair of silver filagree shoe buckles ornamented with delicately wrought roses lay in the folds of paper.

Mary smiled into the brown eyes beside her. "Indeed, I shall think of you, Sir." Then her chin tilted and her lips curled in a saucy smile. "But I shall leave it to your imagination to decide what is in my thoughts."

· 7 ·

Rowland's final term at Cambridge was a steady grind of studying, relieved occasionally by the stimulation of preaching to one of his congregations. On the night of May 18 he wrote in his journal that he had preached in his first barn—and he hoped it might not be his last. The sudden rainshower that attended his meeting caused the farmer to invite all those standing in his field into his barn where, he remarked, their singing might prove soothing to his animals.

The country people were warm in their welcome at Rowland's return. "Been away a long time, young Fella. Ain't 'eard no real preachin' since you been gone." A burly farmer engulfed Rowland's hand in his mighty grasp.

"Sakes alive, it's Mr. 'ill, a-come to preach to us." An old grandmother gave him a toothless grin, then her eyes filled with tears. "I thought not to 'ear ye again."

And Rowland saw with amazement that there were many damp eyes in the hay-scented barn. He knew he had missed his people, but had not known they had missed him so much in return. "The Lord keep you," he replied. "I always find more comfort in speaking to my own people than anywhere else." Whenever Rowland faced discouragement, he always looked for refreshment in the responses of those he preached to. And the greatest discouragement came on those occasions when his preaching provided him with little comfort.

But that was not to be the case this evening, as the barn continued to fill. Rowland's sermon was directly to the people, his

97

examples drawn from things he had seen in the fields or villages. Only one segment of the audience did not respond with favor to such homespun wisdom. A group of gownsmen had interrupted their country ride to join the service that evening.

"Egad! It's Pierrot Hill practicing for his entertainment at Midsummer Faire."

"There is much humor in his performance, but I find his costume somewhat dull."

"Zounds! You've hit upon it! He must be fitted for cap and bells."

Rowland paused and gritted his teeth at the ridicule. His first impulse was to give the gownsmen a good trimming. But instead, he prayed silently for grace to act with forbearance. "If I must be a fool, I would choose to be God's fool," he said quietly, and allowed the words time to sink in before he continued with his preaching.

But the gownsmen were not content to let the matter rest there. Fortified by a supply of port from the public house where they stopped on their way back to the University, they were determined to show who was the fool. Shortly after Rowland returned to his rooms, the sound of banging and calling in his stairwell drew him to open his oak. He was immediately flung back into his apartment by the unruly mob who had come to riot him. He had no more than struggled to his feet and attempted to stop the one nearest him, who was throwing books off the shelf, when help appeared in the form of Bottisham, his cliff-faced visage made awful by the fire in his eyes and the weighty poker he held over his head.

"Zounds! He's called an avenging angel—or demon, more like."

"Damn my eyes! I'll none of it."

"I'm sped!"

They departed as abruptly as they had entered, leaving a wreckage of scattered papers and dumped books behind them, but no material damage to Rowland or his possessions.

"Thank you, Bottisham. Most timely."

The gyp presented him the sturdy metal instrument with an equally poker face. "Might I suggest you lay this in as a weapon of defense, Sir?"

The next day Rowland headed for his lecture a bit hesitantly, wondering if the gang might be lying in wait for further vengeance. Much to his surprise, he was greeted cheerfully by classmates who had barely deigned to nod to him the previous term. Persecution had secured him instant popularity—a status Rowland never thought to achieve at Cambridge.

A student he knew only by sight approached him in New Court. "Sorry to hear you were rioted last night, Hill. Shameless bunch of fellows."

And just outside the lecture hall, Pentycross saluted him. "Hill, I've just heard the news. You all right? Need any help setting your room to rights?"

Rowland assured him that all was well, and that he and Bottisham had everything back in order.

Pentycross grasped his hand once more before hurrying into the lecture. "Can't have any harm come to our best-loved homilist."

Inside the classroom others smiled at him or raised a hand in greeting.

Rowland was completely overcome. How strange that the ostracism he had suffered should suddenly be wiped away, not by any great mark of success on his part, but by one of the most humiliating things that could occur to a gownsman—being rioted in his rooms. It was certainly true that God worked in ways that seemed mysterious to man.

But as the press of studies bore in, Rowland had little time to "assert Eternal Providence and Justify the ways of God to men." As the line from Milton flitted through his mind, he thought of one who had been a most devoted reader of the Puritan poet before her mind was turned to more worldly things. Closing his volume of Locke for an instant, he prayed for Mary.

Pearce, who was tutoring him closely for his degree exams, noticed the waver in Rowland's concentration and brought him back to the second *Treatis on Government*. "State the contract theory of government, Sir."

Rowland rubbed his forehead in an attempt to focus his thoughts on the matter at hand. "The authority of the people is supreme, founded as it is in natural rights. These rights include life, liberty, and property. The people have the right, through their representatives, to judge whether rulers have violated the contract and whether changing times have made a change in government necessary."

"Well done, Hill. You will have no trouble with the examiners." But in spite of his encouraging words, Pearce insisted they continue at the books for an hour longer.

Rowland had no argument with Locke's theories, nor with the requirement to study him; but it never ceased to seem strange to him that in a school of theology, as St. John's purported to be, besides the study of Locke, courses in physics and mathematics bulked the largest. At St. John's even the classics had fallen into great contempt, and honors were based entirely on mathematical ability. What that had to say to preparation for ministry was to be wondered at.

A week later, when the study and exams came to a close, Rowland risked tarnishing his new popularity by declining an invitation to a wine party and went instead to his rooms to write a long overdue letter to his sister Jane.

My Very Dear Sister,

Camb. Tuesday Eve

I ask my dear sister a thousand pardons for not answering her kind letter long before this. All last week almost every moment of my time was taken up in preparing for my degree, which being now over, I'm more at leisure to write.

I was examined by my tutor, then by the senior dean, and then by the junior dean, and then by the Master, who all made me but construe a verse or two apiece in the Greek Testament; except the Master, who asked me both in that and in Plautus and Horace too. I must conclude that my time at Cambridge has not been an intensely intellectual life.

Earnest effort seems to have gone out of the life of the college, as if the loss of religious passions of an earlier generation resulted also in the loss of serious academic endeavors. A college in need of a measure of reform, I should characterize it.

And now but one step remains—ordination. All things continue to give me the safest assurance of an entrance into the ministry by next summer. My heart trembles at the thought of my admission into such an important office. I see myself nothing but ignorance and blindness, utterly unqualified for so great an employment.

If ever I should make an able minister of the New Testament, I see that I must be first wholly given up. I see it requires much grace simply to follow the Lamb wherever He goeth, to

100

forget self, love of ease, and look up to the Glory of God.

I fear much lest my treacherous heart lead me to dissemble. I know that a faithless minister cannot but be a curse instead of a blessing to the church of Christ. Pray for me that Jesus' love may ever constrain me to be faithful unto death.

Therefore my dear sister I must subscribe myself,

yr. poorest tho' affect Br.

Ro Hill

He scattered sand on the ink to dry it, then folded and sealed the document with a blob of blue wax and subscribed the outside to
> Miss Jane Hill
> at Hawkstone
> near Whitechurch
> Shropshire

Then he sat long looking at it, thinking of what he had said. He did fear his heart. He knew the awesome responsibility of his calling—to speak for the mighty God of the universe, Creator of heaven and earth; to call sinners to repentance, that they might spend eternity in the heaven God had created for them. And yet he knew his weakness, his fears.

He was only a man. And next to his longing to serve God, he longed for the companionship of one he had loved for years. In spite of the fact that Charles Wesley's words and example had laid to rest his worst anxieties over Berridge's warnings, he was deeply concerned for Mary. What if she refused him? Or—and a deeper ache caught at his heart—what if she remained in the spiritual confusion she exhibited at Bath? He knew that her religious upbringing had been sound, if rigidly formal, and that her words in their last times together had been spoken in the heat of argument; but he must pray that Mary find her way out of this spiritual wilderness—for her own dear sake, even if she was never to be his wife.

Then one final worry presented itself. What if he should fail the ordination examination? The degree exam had been painless enough, but what if Bishop Sparke should require a depth of learning he had not acquired? He turned again to study his notes from the Sunday afternoon Greek Testament lectures.

And three days later Rowland assembled with fourteen other men of St. John's and other colleges to travel to Ely for examination and admission to Holy Orders. As Rowland looked at those around him, it was obvious that the church attracted every sort of man who came to the college. Some, as one would expect, were sons of clergymen. Others were sizars who had worked their way through college as servants to more privileged students—the attainment of a benefice by way of the University being the most obvious way for a poor man's son to rise in the world. But more than half of the group were, like Rowland, gentlemen's sons.

The group was ushered into a large room in the Bishop's Palace where the Bishop's chaplain, serving as proctor, distributed a separate text to each ordinand with the instructions that he was to write a Latin theme sermonette on the topic. The entire morning passed without a sound in the room except the scratching of fifteen quills across paper. Only two small events provided a break in the protracted concentration. A son of the chaplain came in to talk to his father. And shortly after noon, one of the examinees blurted out, "Egad! I've blotted my page!" crumpled up his paper, threw it to the floor, and began again.

By the time the proctor collected the papers, Rowland's hand ached; but he felt satisfied that he had expressed exactly the right balance of scholarship and practical application in his sermonette. If the rest of the examination went as well, he should soon be a deacon.

At three o'clock the chaplain began ushering the ordinands singly from the room, and a housekeeper served around dishes of tea and slices of spice cake to those still waiting. Hill was the fifth to be called. He followed his guide down a long, polished hallway through double, gothic-arched doors, and into the Presence.

Bishop Sparke sat behind a large, carved desk, lavender and gold streaks of light from the stained glass window behind him falling across his face and the white sleeves of his robe. A slight nod of the eminent head told Rowland which straight-backed chair to sit on. The Bishop picked up his sermonette and read it out aloud. He went straight through without expression or pause. Not another word was spoken.

Rowland bowed and left the room.

When all had been interviewed, they returned to the inn, where relief at having the ordeal over led them to consume vast quantities of roast joint, pudding, and ale. When Rowland finally went up to his room, it was to the sound of his fellow ordinands singing songs that would not be heard in any of the churches they hoped to shepherd.

Rowland slept fitfully. Tomorrow would not be the culmination of all he had dreamed of and worked toward for years—it would be the beginning. He wondered what living would be assigned to him. He didn't care about status; he wanted to serve wherever God could best use him. And the income was of no great concern, for he had a competent allowance from his father; now that he was to be ordained, he needn't fear the patriarchal threat of being cut off. But he did hope the vicarage would be a comfortable one, for Mary's sake. No matter how his rational mind worried him with questions over whether Mary would become his wife, the fact was that he never pictured the future without her.

At last he heard the stirrings of breakfast being prepared below, and he rose and dressed for the day that was to launch his career.

The candidates assembled in the anteroom to the Bishop's private chapel where the ordination service was to take place. The chaplain entered, followed by his son bearing the deacons' mantels which the Bishop would place on their shoulders. The chaplain began calling names and each candidate stepped forward, draped his mantel over his arm, and passed into the chapel. Fourteen names were called. Rowland Hill was not one of them.

The chaplain turned and followed the others into the chapel. His son paused at the door and turned to level a haughty stare at Rowland. "Bishop Sparke is ordaining Anglican deacons, not Methodist enthusiasts."

Rowland had been refused ordination. He stood frozen in the empty chamber as sounds of the beginning service came through the door to the chapel.

He felt amazed that the Bishop had even known. But then he recalled the slightly sneering tone of voice in which the Bishop had pronounced certain words and phrases in his sermonette: regeneration, inspiration, drawing nigh unto God. He had thought that the Bishop's normal voice, but now he knew. He should have taken warning.

He thought of his six friends who had been expelled from

Oxford. Someone had remarked, "If these were expelled for having too much religion, it would be very proper to inquire into the conduct of some who had too little." If he was refused for believing too much, what would become of the ministry of those who were ordained because they believed too little?

He rode back to Cambridge alone. In his stunned condition, his mind would not even let him think of what this would mean to his chances with Mary. And he must consider a specter which loomed even larger at the moment—returning to Hawkstone and facing his family. He must tell his father the consequence of what the Baronet had all along insisted was his son's ruinous fanaticism.

It was night when he reached his rooms, which were blessedly empty as Bottisham didn't expect his return until the next day. Another sleepless night brought him no closer to finding an answer for his future. The question he must settle first in his mind was his own assurance that he had done right. What about his view of a personal God who forgave men their sins individually and filled their hearts with a personal assurance of salvation? A God who listened to impromptu prayers from any sincere heart, no matter how unlearned, and answered those prayers personally? Was this an accurate understanding of God?

Or were such men as Bishop Sparke and Bishop Twysden right? Did God only require a formal assent to the doctrines of the church and take no interest in how man lived his daily life?

After all his struggles, must he acknowledge that the school authorities and his parents and Mary were right? Should he follow in established paths, seek prestigious livings, and rise in the church hierarchy? Was this doing the will of God?

By morning he was no nearer an answer, and could think of only one person to whom he could go for counsel. He had received a note the week before from John Berridge, saying that he would be preaching in Grantchester while staying at the home of a friend; he hoped Rowland could call on him there. Putting on his waistcoat and jacket, sadly rumpled from having been tossed carelessly aside the night before, Rowland suddenly felt better. He hadn't found direction for his life, but he at least had a plan for the rest of the day.

As he crossed the Kitchen Bridge he suddenly became aware of the beauty of the morning, a feeling he would have thought impossible a few hours earlier. The early summer sun sparkled on the waters of the Cam, and the gardens of the Backs shone in green and floral radiance. When the turmoil in his own mind quieted sufficiently for him to listen to the birdsong from elms and willows, he knew that he must believe in a personal God. One who would create so beautiful a world for His creatures' earthly pilgrimage must also care for their eternal souls.

"Hill! Hadn't thought to see you until later today." Simpson and Pentycross crossed the Mathematical Bridge behind Queen's College to join him.

"Forgive me, I should say, Deacon Hill," Pentycross sketched a bow.

Rowland shook his head. This was the part he hated most—having to tell people, "I was refused."

His friends' replies were filled with shock and commiseration. They insisted on bearing him company to call on their old friend. But as they passed the mill and walked on up the shady bank, it seemed that there was no more to say. The silence became heavy and, as the midday sun warmed the air, it became uncomfortably muggy. At last Rowland stopped and without a word, pulled off his coat, shoes, and hat and turned to the river.

Pentycross yelled and made a grab for him when he saw what Rowland was about. "Hill, don't! It's not that final! I say—" But it was too late. Rowland's leg just brushed his friend's hand as he plunged into the river.

"Hill! Hill!" Simpson's voice rose in panic as the water closed over Rowland's head.

The two stood on the bank transfixed in the awfulness of the moment. Then several yards up the river they heard a splashing and a laughing voice calling their names, "Penty! Sim! Bring my clothes. I'll swim to Grantchester."

Rowland turned over on his stomach and struck out with long, sure strokes, which his friends on dry land had no hope of keeping up with.

"Can he do it?" Simpson asked.

Penty nodded. "Oh, yes. I should have realized when I saw him plunge in—strongest swimmer I've ever known—his favorite recreation. But what a crackbrained thing to do at a time like this." Pentycross picked up Rowland's shoes and hat and handed his coat to Simpson.

Rowland emerged dripping and refreshed, if somewhat tired,

from the two-mile swim. And Berridge, who greeted him at the door of William Matthew's home at Grantchester Mill, hardly noticed the unorthodox attire of his young friend, although his housekeeper insisted he have a thorough rubbing with an entire stack of towels before he could be permitted to sit on any of the furniture. By the time Rowland had used the third length of linen, Berridge interrupted the athlete's efforts. "I've a much better idea, my Boy; we'll sit in the garden and let God's sunshine finish the work. Why must man toil and labor when his Maker has provided for all his needs, if he will only look around him?"

When they were settled in the garden, Rowland's companions joined them, looking hot and dusty and much in need of the lemonade the housekeeper was handing around. "Our friend has been telling me of his fellowship with Bishop Sparke," Berridge said.

"In short, he took to me like poison," Rowland concluded.

Berridge smiled at his friend's witticism, but shook his head. "Bishops' powers are very strong indeed—especially in being possessed of the absolute right of conferring orders on whom they choose, without any established regulations.

"When they are once determined no longer to lay their sacred hands on the wicked heads of those whose motives for ordination are the most sacrilegious and impure, and in direct defiance of their most solemn oaths before God, many of those presumptuous intruders into sacred office would seek for their support in some other line, less inconsistent and dishonorable to themselves, and less destructive to the souls of men. Certainly, such a conduct, according to the present corrupted state of things, would procure for their lordships many frowns from the great—but better that than to sustain the eternal frown of God."

All in the circle nodded in somewhat glum agreement at Berridge's summation of the state of things. "But about your present situation, my young Friend, you must simply stand still and not hurry. When the cloud seems to move toward any place, prepare to follow it, and pray to be kept from the delusions of your own spirit and from the wrong counsel of others." Rowland's open look told Berridge much that had not been put into words. "Yes, I see that you have been wrestling with questions of great import since this befell you. Do not let your faith be overset. God is the same yesterday, today, and tomorrow. He will not fail."

Berridge accepted a refill from the housekeeper's pitcher. "Be not anxious about orders. They will come as soon as wanted. Nor be anxious about anything but to know the Lord's will and to do His work. One of your Master's titles is Counselor, and a wonderful Counselor He is. Therefore, take no counsel but of the Lord; so shall you walk more evenly than if you had the whole congregation of Gospel divines at your elbow every moment to advise you."

He smiled as Rowland rubbed at a streak of mud on his breeches. "Your swimming expedition seems a providential prelude for a field preacher this summer."

"Yes!" Rowland brightened visibly. "That is the answer, of course! I must become that which the world despises—a lay itinerant." The words did not seem like cheerful ones, but the twinkle was back in Rowland's eyes. For a few hours he had lost his vision, his sense of God-given mission. But now he knew where the pillar of cloud was leading, and he would gladly follow, convinced of his Lord's blessing. Bees buzzing in the flowering border recalled the allusion Berridge used in his letter to the Countess, and Rowland said, "My desire is to win souls, not livings. If I can secure the bees, I care not who gets the hives."

· 8 ·

IT WAS A TEDIOUS FOUR-DAY JOURNEY by mail coach from Cambridge to Shrewsbury, each day made more uncomfortable because Rowland was nearer to facing his father. He had intended to hire a horse at Shrewsbury to carry him the remaining way to Hawkstone, but as the coach rattled up to the inn, he caught a glimpse of his brother Richard going in to take his afternoon meal. "Richard! Well met!" In the instant joy of seeing Richard, Rowland forgot the bad news he bore with him like a dark cloud. Berridge's words and his own sense of calling had cheered him, but he knew they would mean little to the rest of his family, even to those who supported him and had great faith in his future.

Richard clasped Rowland's hand warmly, then picked up two of his brother's valises and led the way into the coaching house.

"Why didn't you write that you were coming? Jane will be beside herself with delight. She's been having a bad time of it; Mother's not well and all the nursing falls on her." Richard interrupted himself to direct the landlord to send their meals to the private parlor he always used when in Shrewsbury. They settled themselves in comfortable chairs on either side of the table.

"You're unaccountably quiet, Rowly. So what living were you given? The Bishop send you to Northumberland until you learn some manners, did he?"

"The Bishop sent me to Jericho."

Richard was stunned. "What? You were *refused?* What will you do?"

The question hung in the air as the serving girl entered with a

108

hearty pork pie and platters of rabbit stew. Rowland, whose troubles seldom dulled his appetite, took a wide wedge of pie and did justice to several bites, followed by a long drink of cider before he answered.

"I shall preach."

Richard shook his head. "I admire you. I must tell you that I have bent to our Father's persuasion and am no longer preaching. As the heir, I let myself be convinced to exhibit my Christianity in other ways."

Rowland frowned. "Were you directly forbidden?"

"Not quite, but I could see it would soon come to it. And with Mother's health so poor, it seemed best."

Rowland nodded. "Perhaps for a time. But I could no more stop preaching than I could stop breathing. I'm sure if I were to do the one, it would lead to the other. If ever you hear I have ceased sermonizing, send a note round to the coffin maker." Rowland ate the tender white meat off a bone before he continued. "I have been thinking much of the letters you wrote me at Eton. Do you recall them?"

Richard shrugged. "I remember writing them, certainly, and encouraging your fledgling faith. I hope they may have done some good. It would be a shame if the amount of ink and paper that was expended on the project, to say nothing of the candlewax, should come to nothing. But I don't recall any of my words exactly."

"I have the advantage of you, Richard. I have kept them all and reread them from time to time. Their language is worthy of a preacher. 'Consider, my dear Brother, how that when you as a poor helpless sheep were gone astray, this dear Shepherd sought you and brought you back. Remember how, when wandering further and further from His fold, He made you hear His voice and follow Him, carrying you as a lamb in His bosom and gently leading you whilst you were yet young.' That is an image that I have dwelt on often in time of trial."

"I wrote that, did I? Yes, it does have a nice turn of phrase, and the doctrine is sound. Do you recall more?"

"A bit. 'Think of this love which passeth knowledge, and may it fill your heart with praise, and your tongue with thanksgiving. Let it constrain you to live to Him who died for you, and to grow daily more and more in conformity to His blessed image, that so you may adorn the doctrine of God our Saviour in all things, and by

109

welldoing, put to silence the ignorance of foolish men, who would falsely accuse your good conversation in Christ.' That is what I have endeavored to do, Richard."

Richard was thoughtful for some time. "With such fortification you shall succeed. But convincing our parents of the rightness of the matter will be quite another affair."

A few hours later, Richard's carriage rolled through the large tract of rocks and woods that made the entrance to Hawkstone. Unlike the gently wooded, rolling green estates to be found over much of England, the Hill lands were composed of steep rocky outcroppings interspersed with woods, patches of undergrowth and bushes, then crannies of stone where oaks of uncommon magnitude seemed to be growing from the rocks themselves.

Rowland, who had always thought the landscape most appropriate for their family name, couldn't refrain from hoping that on this occasion it was not symbolic of the reception he would encounter.

Then around the final sweep, Hawkstone House came into view. The pale stone mansion, set on the side of a hill, glowed like Roman marble in the dusk, its many columns, arches, and classical proportions giving support to the allusion. From the center of the house, Palladian wings curved forward on either side, a one-story portico connecting higher sections and then coming to a graceful conclusion by rooms of lower elevation again. The roof of the central mansion and the lower connecting sections was adorned with rows of classical stone urns which at that moment were tinted red by the dying rays of light.

"Welcome back to the noble pile." Richard handed Rowland's bags to the groom who came out to meet them. "But don't expect a fatted calf. Not that Jane wouldn't have put one on, if she'd known you were coming."

But Jane had seen from an upstairs window and now came running to welcome "her dear little Rowly" with open arms.

"Dear Jane, it's so good to see you, but you look fatigued. Richard said you've been nursing Mother much of late." He returned her embrace and fond greetings, then held his sister at arm's length and surveyed her. "Can't someone help you? Have you written to Elizabeth?"

"Oh, yes. I have done so. But caring for our mother is not the wearying thing." Jane paused with a sigh. We are a house divided against itself. When will it ever end, Rowland? It is inexpressibly

110

painful that our dear parents, so worthy of honor in every other relation except in that having to do with our Christian obligations, should be so desperately misled."

"What? Jane, has our father become despotic? I never found him so."

Jane, who as the at-home, elder daughter of the thirteen Hill children, oversaw the housekeeping duties, led Rowland to his room. "No, no. He is never unjust. Oh, there are occasional explosions of his wrath, to be sure, but I am not constrained to refrain from practicing my faith. It is just that the years of internal warfare, with those who in every other light are so loved, and I am so desirous of pleasing, is sometimes unutterably wearing."

"Dear Jane," Rowland took his sister in his arms. "You have always stood a second mother to me, from the time you taught me my letters. I would I could help you, but I fear I have only come to add to your burden."

"No, Rowland. How is that possible?"

Rowland looked her clearly in the eyes and got the announcement over with as briefly as possible. "I must tell you that I have been refused ordination."

Far from the shock and disbelief the news had produced in others, Jane, in her commonsense way was entirely unmoved. "Then you must apply elsewhere. The Bishop of Ely is not the be-all and end-all of ordination powers."

Rowland smiled. "Jane, Jane. What a tonic you are. It's no wonder we all look to you to hold the family together. I shall take your advice and apply to the next Bishop I encounter."

Alfred, Sir Richard's first footman who always acted as Mr. Rowland's man when he was home, unpacked for him. After a brief look-in on his mother to let her know he had arrived and to wish her a speedy recovery, Rowland had one final duty which could no longer be delayed.

The study was in a far corner of Hawkstone House, so Rowland had plenty of time to dread his father's reaction as he made his way through the marble-floored halls with their ornately plastered walls. Sir Richard's library was a spacious room with high arched windows, fine marble fireplace, and floor-to-ceiling books that could be reached by a wheeled stepladder. He sat at his desk going over some estate papers, but at Rowland's entrance, he came forward.

"Ah, Rowland, welcome home. I had word of your arrival, but knew you would call on your mother first. How do you find her this evening?"

Rowland's eyes were sad. "Fearfully reduced, Sir. What does Dr. Fansham say?"

"Nothing much to the purpose. "But tell me of yourself, Son. You have taken your degree?"

"Yes, Sir, but—"

"Come, come. Let us not stand upon ceremony, but sit in comfort." Sir Richard resumed his seat at his desk and Rowland sat in an upholstered chair nearby.

His father was silent, so Rowland forged ahead. "I was denied orders, Sir."

The silence hung heavy in the room, Sir Richard's features immobile. Then he clapped his hands together so sharply Rowland jumped. "Well, that's fine. Sparke did quite right. Now that you've seen the error of your ways, you can renounce your irregular enthusiasms and receive ordination from Bishop Exley. I'll have a word with him about it—just a hint that youthful follies are to be readily forgiven. You mother and I shall be very proud of you; you'll rise high in the church once your foot is set on the right course. Shouldn't be surprised to see you a bishop yourself someday."

Rowland looked at the floor. This reaction was far worse than if his father had burst out in anger. Slowly raising his head, he looked his father in the eyes. "No, Father. I do not renounce my belief in a personal God, nor my determination to preach the Gospel thereof."

Now the anger Rowland had expected from the first broke. "What! You mean to continue in this disastrous way? Have you no common sense? Are you all stubbornness? How bitter it is to have an ungrateful son—more bitter far than the sting of an adder."

"Please Father, I am not ungrateful for all you have done for me. You've always been most generous. But neither can I be ungrateful for what God has done for me. Even with all you have provided, His mercy has been greater. I cannot refuse what He would have me do. 'How can we prosper if we refuse so great a salvation?' "

Again, Sir Richard was silent. Then he said, "I do not comprehend this—that my son should be openly counted among the pub-

112

licans and sinners, one of the curiosities of the day. It is hard enough to have Richard and your sister Jane share this Methodistical bias, but they do so quietly, whereas you are making a public figure of yourself and leading others into your way."

"I hope so, Father. To lead others is my calling." Rowland spoke the words quietly, so as to give no hint of disrespect.

"Leave me now. I shall speak further to you on this matter at a later date. Try not to upset your mother."

Rowland bowed and took his leave.

The next day after breakfast, Rowland was drawn by the summer sun shining on Shropshire's green rugged hills to take a walk around Hawkstone's fields and call on their tenants. He had gone only so far as the bottom of the field, however, when he realized word of his arrival had run ahead of him and a large number of his father's tenants, as well as people from the village, had come to greet him.

To Rowland, a crowd in a field meant just one thing—a congregation to be preached to. So after a few minutes of chatting with folk he had known since childhood, and inquiring after their various ills and numerous family members, he jumped up on a large boulder in a corner of the pasture.

"Friends, if you will it, I shall preach to you."

A cheer went up from the crowd—a rare experience for a field preacher who was always far more likely to be egged or pelted with mud clods than cheered. "You allus told me yer stories when ye were a wee lad," an old shepherd bent over his stick called out. "And right fine stories they allus were. Tell us another now, Lad."

The crowd agreed, and Rowland, who never read his sermons anyway, and now found himself without even a Bible in his hands, looked around for inspiration. Seeing the path across the sheep-dotted hillside which he had thought to follow for his morning ramble, he began. "Some of you may think I am preaching a rambling sermon, but if I should be able to reach the heart of a poor rambling sinner, I'm sure you'll forgive me. My friends, you may ramble from Christ, but He will ramble after you and try to bring you back into His fold."

His hearers laughed at the homely allusion and called hearty encouragement to the speaker.

But back in the study at Hawkstone House, the unusual sound met the ears of Sir Richard who hastily dispatched a footman to

113

bring Richard to him. His heir arrived in a matter of minutes during which time several more such disturbing sounds reached the study led by one clear, male voice with exceptional carrying quality.

"Richard, I wish you would tell me—whose voice is that assaulting my ears?"

Richard was quiet and listened for a moment. "Why, sir, that is Rowland, preaching to the people in the neighborhood."

Sir Richard was neither surprised nor pleased. "Go, tell him to come to me." Richard started to turn for the door. "Immediately!" his father added.

Richard was no more than halfway across the wide green Hawkstone lawn when he could hear Rowland's words distinctly. "I cannot fathom with my puny understanding the mystery of the divine decrees. I can only say with St. Paul, 'O the depth of His riches!' We know nothing—can any man tell me *why* grass is green?" Rowland drew a wide arc with his arm, encompassing all the emerald hillside. As his hand swept across the path, he saw his brother approaching. He knew instantly why Richard was coming, but continued the thought he was developing. "Then let us leave all *explanations* and simply believe what God has revealed.

"My friends, think on these matters for a moment, search your hearts and we will speak more on the matter." He turned to Richard who now stood at the foot of the rock.

"Our father bids you come to him—immediately."

"What shall I do with the congregation?" Rowland directed Richard's gaze to the crowd who now numbered close to fifty. "I cannot go, unless you come up and finish my discourse."

Rowland jumped down from his granite pulpit and Richard, with an amused grin at his brother, climbed up. Rowland walked quickly along the path, hearing Richard's quieter voice urging the farm laborers to follow the Good Shepherd.

Sir Richard was ready for his erring son with the lecture on irregular conduct that was to be expected. "You pray without the Book of Common Prayer, hold what are termed evangelical sentiments, and preach to a mixed multitude of people in unconsecrated places. Bishop Exley will never ordain you. I shouldn't even ask him." He broke off his colloquium as a new sound came through the open windows. "I hear some other person preaching. Who is that?"

"I suppose it is Richard, finishing my sermon, Sir."

Sir Richard banged a fist on his desk. "Go immediately and tell him I command him to come at once to me." Rowland took an obedient step toward the door. "And do you come with him."

By the time Rowland reached the bottom of the field, however, Richard had finished the discourse and dismissed the congregation. Both brothers returned to their father who continued the reprimand he had been issuing to Rowland, now with doubled vigor as he had two heads to ring the peal over. "You are degrading yourselves by preaching in the open air without so much as aid of a proper pulpit."

Sir Richard paused for breath and Richard dared a quick allusion. "But, surely, Father, trained in the law as you are, you can see the precedent." He paused, but not long enough for an answer. "Our sermon was on a mount, just as our Lord's example of field preaching."

Sir Richard's mouth was open to continue his lecture, but his son's shot was so apropos he sat with his mouth open and no words coming out.

Rowland was quick to take up the advantage. "And Father, our words were much appreciated. Old Molly from the dairy told me it was the finest preaching she had ever heard. I would have been much complimented, if I didn't know Molly has been stone-deaf these twenty years." Sir Richard's gape turned to the merest shadow of a smile. "And Crooker's wife listened the whole time with a young lamb in her arms. It was impossible to tell which had the broader smile, she or the lamb." Rowland said.

And Richard took up his story, "And as the lamb hasn't yet grown any teeth and Mrs. Crooker has lost all of hers, they made a fine twin set."

Sir Richard relaxed into a smile. "Well, I am pleased that the people in the vicinity of my mansion should be kept in good humor."

The sons, knowing when they had pressed their advantage far enough, bowed and retired.

It was late that evening when the sound of carriage wheels on the graveled drive brought Rowland, Richard, and Jane to the front steps of Hawkstone House. Rowland, who had seen it recently in Bath, was the first to recognize Clement's coach-and-four. "Here's support for you, Jane; our sister Elizabeth has arrived."

115

With a glad cry, Jane rushed forward to greet her sister with open arms. Elizabeth hugged all her family members roundly before Rowland realized that the footman was handing another lady out of the carriage.

Mary Tudway emerged, shaking the wrinkles from her blue traveling dress with one hand and holding a well-brushed Spit in the other. As Rowland stepped forward to welcome Mary, Spit saw his rescuer from the gutters of Bath and with a glad, shrill yap, leapt from Mary's arm straight to Rowland's. Fortunately, Rowland was nimble in the catching, but the unexpectedness of it caused him to step backwards, treading on the hem of Elizabeth's full skirt, and adding a sharp tearing sound to the rest of the noisy greeting.

"Sir, if you were not my brother I should rap you severely for such an affront."

"I beg your pardon, Sister, but it was your back."

It was not until after dinner, which the Baronet always ordered served in midafternoon, that Rowland had opportunity to talk to Mary alone. "I am so pleased you have borne my sister company. Both for her sake and my own. I had not hoped to see you for some time yet."

As he spoke the words, Rowland knew he was happy to see Mary; but it bore in upon him, more sharply than anything yet had done, the unenviable position he was in. This was the time he had looked forward to as being able to make Mary an offer. Here she was, unexpectedly, delightfully, at Hawkstone, holding his arm as he led her on a walk around the grounds, and he could speak of nothing but the landscape.

It seemed now that he would be forever debarred from speaking what was in his heart. "Would you prefer to sit in the summer-house or to visit the grotto?"

"Oh, I should far prefer the grotto. And Elizabeth told me you have a hermit cave and a castle ruin. What a perfect setting for the *Castle of Oranto!*"

Rowland laughed at her allusion. "Yes, and the eminent Dr. Johnson would agree with you. After his visit here he wrote to our father that he found Hawkstone quite marvelous. 'It excels in the extent of its prospects, the awfulness of its shades, the horrors of its precipices, the verdure of its hollows, and the loftiness of its rocks. The ideas which it forces upon the mind are the sublime, the dreadful, and the vast. Above is inaccessible attitude, below is horrible profundity. He that mounts the precipices at Hawkstone wonders how he came thither, and doubts how he shall return. His walk is an adventure, and his departure an escape.' "

"O Sir, you have stimulated my appetite for adventure beyond all bounds. Lead the way, I pray."

They started with the grotto, a large oval cavern hewn in the rocky hillside behind the house. It had been cut far into the rock, and pillars chiseled in imitation of stalagmites and stalagtites supported its winding recesses.

"Can we go in?" Mary stood on a boulder on the downhill side of the stream issuing from the grotto and peered into the stone chamber.

"If you are very careful. I did it often as a child. But I fear for your skirts."

"Oh, fah. What consequence are they when such an adventure offers?"

Rowland leapt across the stream and extended his hand to Mary to steady her jump to the stone ledge forming the floor of the grotto. Her jump was strong, but she was not prepared for the slickness of the damp stone. As her feet slipped from under her, she gave a small cry and reached out to Rowland. The black rocks were rushing up to meet her when Rowland's strong arms scooped her up and set her firmly on the solid rock. She clung to him. Nor did he release his hold on her, but drew her closer. There was no resistance as his adored Mary settled in his arms. He dropped his head to hers, his lips in her hair, bared by the hat that had fallen to the rocks in the mishap. She smelled of lavender essence. "Mary—" He dropped his lips to her cheek, with every intention of going further to find her lips. But the sound of his own voice, echoing in the rocky cave, brought an awareness of where they were, who they were, and the enormous impropriety of what he was about. And worse, the fact that he would likely never have the right to hold her so.

"Mary." He pushed her away from him, retaining hold only on one arm to steady her. "Forgive me. I have in the past indicated to you my feelings, but I did not mean to—I would never—forgive me for—"

Mary laughed. "La, Sir. What a fuss you make. Forgive you for rescuing your sister-in-law from a nasty fall on the rocks? What gentleman would beg forgiveness for such an act? Should I have preferred you to allow me to dash myself on the stones?"

Rowland smiled his appreciation of her easing the situation, and they left the grotto and continued their tour on toward the Red Castle ruin. An ancient pile remained of a medieval fortress built of the local iron-rich clay. Only one tower and three walls of the keep remained, of what had once been a mighty structure. Ivy grew over most of the fallen stones. Rowland cleared a space on a seat in what had once been the Great Hall and spread his linen handkerchief for Mary to sit on.

But, that activity accomplished, he could not bring himself to tell her what he must; so instead he asked, "And how are your family in Wells?"

"All are well in Wells, Sir," she answered with a straight face and Rowland laughed appreciatively.

"And events?"

"If I said as dull as ditchwater you would accuse me of deplorable humor, so I shall desist. The answer, however, would be quite accurate. For lack of anything else, I have returned to the activity I hate most in this world—making embroidered seat covers."

"Do you not read?"

"Ah, yes, I have read and reread *Humphrey Clinker*. Its delightful descriptions of Bath only sink me deeper by making me miss the pleasures I once knew." She turned aside and looked out over the evening-shadowed expanse as she quoted,

"All is gayety, good humor, and diversion. The eye is continually entertained with the splendor of dress and equipage; and the ear with the sound of coaches, chaises . . . the merry bells . . . the singing of the waits. We have music in the Pump Room every morning, cotillions every forenoon in the rooms, balls twice a week, and concerts every other night, besides private assemblies and parties without number."

And Rowland wondered if she were also missing Roger, but he only asked, "And is that truly the life you would choose, Mary?"

A sigh escaped her. "I don't know. I think so when I recall the pleasures. But at the time, I found it palled a bit. One must have *something* to do, however, and if I am required to accomplish any more needlework, I shall needs be clapped in Bedlam. Elizabeth has invited me to accompany her to London when they remove there, but it is months until Parliament opens."

"And in London you will seek more pleasures?"

"What else is there? The opera, the theatre, Ranelagh and Vauxhall."

If Rowland had been disspirited when he began this conversation, every word Mary spoke made his prospects look more dismal. "But Mary, you could find occupation of more lasting importance."

She gave a brittle laugh. "La, what do you suggest, Sir? That I take up field preaching?"

A new idea struck him. "Mary, next week I go to preach to congregations near Welshampton and Ellesmere. Would you accompany me?"

"If I don't have to take my embroidery with me."

Her light answer would have been a happy conclusion to the conversation if there were not one more matter yet to discuss. "I shall be particularly glad of your company, Mary. You see, I may be obliged to spend a rather long time engaged in field preaching."

"Nonsense, Rowland. You have taken your degree. Won't you pass on to orders soon? I had thought you might already have done so. Maria, whose father is a Canon, told me it is often done immediately upon taking degrees. What—"

Rowland cut into her monologue. "Yes. For all but one of our number it was so."

Rowland was becoming accustomed to the shocked silence which always followed this intelligence.

After a moment Mary clasped her hands firmly together and said in a decided voice, "Then, Sir, you must abandon your irregularities. I did warn you it would be so. Now you must see—"

Rowland's voice was equally firm. "I did not expect that of you, Mary. It is the advice of a coward. When we are afraid and begin to shrink back, the devil knows he is gaining ground. I cannot bear flying away and turning my back—there is no armor given for the back."

"Are all who are not fanatics cowards? I don't ask you to give up your religion or your preaching, just your enthusiasm."

Always fond of making his point by telling a story, Rowland's eyes twinkled for the first time since the conversation turned serious. "Because I am in earnest, men call me an enthusiast. But I am not a zealot; mine are the words of truth and soberness. Three summers ago I was walking on yonder hill," he said, and pointed to the west where a rocky hill rose in the middle distance. "I saw a gravel pit fall in and bury three human beings alive. I lifted up my voice for help so loud that I was heard in the town below, at a distance of a mile. Help came and rescued two of the poor sufferers. No one called me an enthusiast then. And when I see eternal destruction ready to fall upon poor sinners, and about to entomb them irrecoverably in an eternal mass of woe, and call aloud on them to escape, shall I be called an enthusiast now?"

Mary gave no reply, but the furrow to her brow showed that she was considering his words.

"When you come with me next week, you shall see and may judge the matter for yourself."

Mary was quiet on the return walk, like the thoughtful girl Rowland had known her to be before the frivolities of Bath and Sarah Child's example turned her head to more worldly things. Rowland ached for the meditative companion she had once been to him. He knew that whatever turn her mind took, he would always love Mary Tudway, and he prayed that God might direct her mind and heart in ways he was incapable of doing.

Later in her room, Mary knew a similar conflict. Rowland's words made sense, and yet she could not accept them, could not think that his way was right. She wrestled with the matter until her head ached; then, determined to find lighter amusement, she picked up *Humphrey Clinker*. She smiled at the servant girl's letter to her friend back home.

O Molly! You that live in the country have no deception of our doing at Bath. Here is such dressing, and fiddling, and dancing, and gadding, and courting, and plotting—O gracious! If God had not given me a good stock of discretion, what a power of things might not I reveal.

The amusing pictures those words called to mind made Mary relax, and her head ceased to ache. She read on through a few more letters of the novel until she came to one from an Oxford student.

London itself can hardly exhibit one species of diversion to which we have not something analogous at Bath . . . and daily opportunities of seeing the most remarkable characters of the community. One sees them in their natural attitudes and true colors, descended from their pedestals, and divested of their formal draperies, undisguised by art and affectation. . . . There is always a great show of the clergy at Bath, waddling like so many crows along the North Parade. None of your thin, puny, yellow, hectic figures, exhausted with abstinence and hard study, but great, overgrown dignitaries and rectors, with rubicund noses and gouty ankles—the emblems of sloth and indigestion.

For a moment Mary could see nothing but Bishop Twysden in his gorgeous robes, sipping claret in the Countess' Nicodemus Chamber.

Was this truly what she wanted for Rowland? Should he abandon his passion for God and the souls of men for the sake of money and honor? And yet, what if no Bishop could be found to ordain him? Would he spend his life in a field? A Baronet's son?

And if he obtained ordination and a living, and spoke the words to her he had so long hinted at, what would her answer be? There was no doubting her pleasure in his company; but would she be a worthy wife for a man of such serious calling? Shouldn't he take a more serious wife to whom doing good came naturally—like Lady Selina? But such musings did nothing to the point of answering her question to herself—would *she* make a fit wife for Rowland Hill?

If he were to be anything but a clergyman, she knew that she wouldn't hesitate. Every occasion with him taught her heart more clearly what was truly in it. But having a good time was very important to her. She couldn't live as pious Lady Huntingdon did. If that was how she'd have to be . . . she shuddered. But if she were to refuse him, if life were to hold no more pleasant times with Rowland—her throat closed and her eyes filled with tears at the thought.

And then Rowland's twinkling eyes filled her mind. He wasn't a long-faced ascetic, and she doubted he would want her to be one either.

Still in the mood of serious reflection, she turned to her old favorite, Milton. But she didn't find his sonnet on the brevity

121

of youth to be of much comfort.

> How soon hath Time, the subtle thief of youth,
> Stolen on his wing my three-and-twentieth year!
> My hasting days fly on with full career,
> But my late spring no bud of blossom shew'th.
> Perhaps my semblance might deceive the truth,
> That I to manhood am arrived so near;
> And inward ripeness doth much less appear,
> That some more timely-happy spirits endu'th.
> Yet it be less or more, or soon or slow,
> It shall be still in strictest measure even
> To that same lot, however mean or high,
> Toward which Time lead me, and the will of heaven:
> All is, if I have grace to use it so,
> As ever in my great Taskmaster's eye.

If only she could have Milton's confidence that after her twenty years of accomplishing little more than three embroidered seat cushions, she could do something truly splendid.

· 9 ·

THE FOLLOWING WEEK not even the drizzling August rain could dampen Mary's sense of adventure as she set out in Sir Richard's closed carriage with coronets on the door. Surely no one had ever been more elegantly conducted to a field service. Elizabeth's Minson sat on the seat facing her, holding Spit on a cushion on her lap. The little dog, usually a comfortable, sleepy creature, today sat alert, his ears perked, watching everything outside the carriage window. Raindrops on the windowpane dimmed Mary's view of the Shropshire fields, some more green than ever in the rain, some the soft gold of ripening wheat.

She had argued without success that it was quite ridiculous for Rowland to ride in the rain when he could just as well sit dry and comfortable in his father's carriage. But he merely laughed and replied that he shouldn't shrink with a little wetting—and it might not be such a bad thing if he did. And besides, the experience would be useful if he chose to preach a sermon on Noah.

Accompanying a field-preaching circuit was something Mrs. Tudway would have been unlikely to grant permission for her daughter to do; but as Elizabeth held a degree of sympathy for her young brother's activity, and was far too occupied in nursing her mother to give the matter much attention other than ordering Minson to accompany Mary, there was no one to forbid the excursion.

As they drove northwestward toward the Welsh border, the scenery became more mountainous and more intensely green. After traveling some miles in a narrow, cultivated valley between

123

wooded mountains, Mary could see the descent into the vale in which they would meet the first congregation. The vale was a succession of gentle hills carefully cultivated by Marcher farmers. The Afton Dyfrdwy wound through it, a tiny blue line; on the declivity of a mountain about a mile away stood a castle.

Mary felt there could be no more beautiful country in the world than this Welsh borderland. She wanted to drive on and on, deeper into this land she had never seen before. She had heard of the majesty and ruggedness of the mountains in Wales—and this was only a foretaste. She leaned forward on the carriage seat and pressed her face against the window. Rowland saluted her with a wave and a smile, and Mary suddenly discovered that the country could be quite as exciting as the city.

After a night passed pleasantly at a rustic but comfortable inn, the party rose at five o'clock and drove a few miles northward toward Wrexham where Rowland planned to address his first congregation. He told Mary he had chosen to begin there because he had preached in that area before and knew the people to be friendly and receptive. After all, field preaching didn't always attract the mildest of audiences. As soon as Mary saw the sun rise over the mountains, she felt sure this would be a happy day. It was impossible to think of anything going amiss in this world.

As the carriage slowed to a stop at the spot where Rowland knew people from nearby villages would be passing on their way to market, Mary saw another delightful scene. At first it appeared that giant spiders had been busily spinning through the night, as an entire field was covered with fine white thread glowing silver in the morning light. "That field!" Mary pointed toward the silver light as Rowland helped her descend from the carriage.

"A tenterfield," Rowland said. "The women of the villages use it to dry their yarn. Be sure Spit doesn't try to run in it. Neither he nor the women would be happy with the job of untangling him."

Rowland walked to the edge of the field and spoke to the women guarding it, inviting them to attend his service. They unlatched the gate to the field and followed him back to the stile he would use as a platform. Soon several laborers from neighboring fields, a group of dairymaids, and some families on their way to market had gathered around the preacher. It seemed to Mary almost a matter of magic, that as soon as Rowland began preaching, his crowd of twenty listeners multiplied to forty and upwards. She thought fleetingly of the miracle of the loaves and fishes and smiled. She couldn't wait to tell Rowland—he always liked commonplace illustrations, and she had found one for him.

Three county lads driving a pack of pigs stopped at the back of the crowd and let their charges root in the grass, while they leaned on their staves and listened to the preacher who had apparently drawn his inspiration from the basket of eggs a young woman carried on her arm. "Oftentimes, when I have been engaged in field preaching, I have thought a whole village to be dead in trespasses and sins. But then, success for the work of God came from a few quiet ones whom I left like a nest of eggs." He pointed to the girl's basket and she blushed with pleasure. "When I visited them again, the numbers had increased, so that the little nest of eggs became a healthy brood.

"Now, I ask you to look into your own hearts. How many of you—"

The preacher's words were drowned out by the most dreadful squall Mary had ever heard: squeaking, grunting, and snorting followed by sharp, frantic female screams. Spit, secure in Mary's arms, added his yapping to the din, and without knowing what was amiss, the entire congregation turned to follow the sound of the disturbance. When Mary reached the fence, she couldn't help laughing.

The pigs, left to their own devices by their drivers, had wandered into the tenterfield which the women, in their hurry to attend the meeting, had left unbarred. Five fat, pink-and-black porkers had gotten their snout rings entangled in the yarn, and the more they shook their heads to free themselves, the more they became imprisoned.

It was impossible to say which made more noise, the women bemoaning the calamity to their yarn, the drivers shouting at their pigs, the congregation who had found a better entertainment than the preacher, or the frightened and enraged pigs. But it was the women who took the matter in hand. Each one grasped a hog by a back leg, and throwing her weight against the broadside of the pig, turned it on its back; then, straddling the animal to keep it capsized, she began to disentangle the muddy head from the twine— to the accompaniment of cheers and clapping from the crowd.

Rowland took Mary's arm and turned her toward the carriage. "I know when I've been outdone. There'll be no more preaching here today."

Mary hoped he wouldn't be disheartened by his aborted service; but when he had tethered his horse to the back of the carriage and joined Mary and Minson inside, he exploded in laughter so full the carriage rocked on its springs. "I had to get away before I disgraced myself by laughing!"

"Why should you, who are noted for your humor, not laugh?"

Rowland shook his head and dabbed his eyes. "It's one thing to make people laugh. It's another to do it yourself. I wouldn't want to become characterized as a Laughing Parson, even though I do hope to counteract the current notion that wit is wicked and humor sinful. Or that dullness is holy, and solemn stupidity is full of grace." He reached up and rapped sharply on the roof of the carriage as a signal to the coachman to drive on. "If dullness were a divine power, the world would have been converted by now."

After a few miles Rowland signaled the driver to stop, he would continue the journey as outrider. "We should have a large meeting across the border at Garth. I have preached there many times and they have put up notices of my coming. I want to think how I can liken our pigs in the tenterfield to the story of the Gadarene demoniac."

That evening it seemed that, indeed, the entire town of Garth had been informed of Rowland Hill's coming. When Mary saw the size of the congregation, she was delighted that he should be given such a welcome. But he had no more than mounted the haywain that stood at the top of the field for his use as a platform, than such a din began that it made the morning's cacophony seem a hymn-sing by comparison. It might be that some had come to welcome him, but most were there to exercise their right to make sport of field preachers and had come armed with pans, shovels, buckets—anything of tin or iron that could be beat upon. Others were blowing horns and ringing bells. For a moment Mary hoped the din might be some sort of welcoming band; but when she saw Rowland pelted with eggs and mud, she knew the truth of their intentions. And she knew too the truth of her feelings. She wanted to leap on the wagon and fling herself in front of him, to protect him from the degrading missiles. She wanted to tell that rag-mannered mob just what she thought of them that they should dare to treat this fine man in such a way. She wanted—but Spit began yapping shrilly and struggling in her arms so that she became aware of her

126

own voice. And with red-faced alarm, she realized that the things she wanted to do she had actually done in a fine burst of temper.

"Rowland Hill has come here at considerable discomfort to himself so you can hear the Word of God. And this is the way you treat him! He'd be far better off preaching to a flock of sheep or a field of stones; they'd be more polite and they'd get just as much out of it as you would acting like this!"

Spit caught her fervor and barked an emphatic punctuation to each sentence.

Whether it was her outraged action or Spit's fine performance that carried the day she couldn't tell, but the crowd was suddenly quiet. Rowland stepped to her side, wiping a blob of egg off his cheek. "Thank you, Mary. Stay with me," he said in her ear, then turned to the audience. "I see we are a band of music lovers gathered here tonight."

The crowd roared with laughter. "Now, it's exceedingly fine to love music—but it's important to understand the difference between music and noise. If you will, I'll show you how we can work together and turn this hubbub into harmony."

Not a murmur was heard in the field as they waited to hear what the preacher had to say. "This fine lady, Miss Tudway, has come all the way from Wells." The fact that few in the crowd knew where Wells was made the announcement more impressive. "And she is going to help me lead in singing Charles Wesley's hymn, 'Blessed be the Name.' Now, here's what I want you to do. Those of you with—er, drums, will mark the rhythm. Those with bells will ring them on the phrase, 'Blessed be the name of the Lord!' and those with horns will blow them at the end of each phrase. Now, let's try it!"

Mary sang her heart out, trying to add a bit of real melody to what was only a slightly more organized version of the earlier din. The thumping and banging accompanied, "O for a thousand tongues to sing" followed by an ear-splitting blast from the horns; then "Blessed be the name of the Lord!" could just be heard above a jangle of bells.

The results left Mary, who had a strong but untrained voice, wishing heartily she had not been so adamant in begging to be allowed to discontinue her music lessons. But the mob loved it and Rowland good-naturedly led them on through succeeding verses. "Jesus, the name that charms our fears," with a blare of trumpets and ending with a final, triumphant, "Blessed be the name of the Lord!" that left everyone panting for breath.

"And I'm sure the angels are applauding you right now!" Rowland congratulated his audience as he handed Mary down off the makeshift platform. "Now, my audiences almost always listen to me while standing up in the field; but as you've worked so hard, I'd like to invite you to sit right down in God's green grass, while I tell you a story." After they were settled Rowland told of their morning's porcine encounter. He went on to recount the story from Mark 5, of Jesus casting out a legion of demons from the possessed man and then granting their request that He not send them out of the country but allow them to enter a herd of swine. "Now, I'm not suggesting that those pigs this morning were demon-possessed, though you might have thought so to hear the ruckus they set up. What I want you to notice from this story is that Jesus did this because those demons asked Him to. Now, if Jesus would grant the request of demons, just think how much more readily He will grant the prayers of His children."

The anger and antagonism of an hour before was completely gone, and a sense of relaxed warmth pervaded the meadow. The setting sun painted the western sky pink and gold, more elegant than any stained-glass window; and Mary, who could never before have imagined worshiping without a prayer book in her hand and a prayer rail at which to kneel, looked around her. She noted the richness of Rowland's voice, the ease with which his words came, and the good sense they spoke to her heart. She saw how much Rowland's preaching meant to him, and how right he was for the task, even if no bishop could be convinced to formalize his position.

That night, over a late supper at the inn, Mary tried to convey some of her feelings to Rowland. "I understand much better now what you've tried to tell me. I won't say I've been wrong to urge you to seek a less irregular path, but I do have a better idea of the force of your preaching."

He looked at her in the firelit room. "And, Mary, if circumstances arrange themselves so that our paths become—ah, closer, can you be content to see me despised and rejected in my Master's service?"

She dropped her head. That was the crucial question. And she didn't know the answer. A day ago she would have thought an affirmative impossible. But after her quick, protective action that evening, where for a moment she had entered as wholly as he into the service—she finished her meal in silence.

"Go have Minson tuck you in bed." Rowland smiled at her. "We have just one service tomorrow, and then I must return you to my sister."

As they drove toward Oswestry the next day, Mary couldn't help wishing that the meeting might be sparsely attended. And the fact that the rain seemed to be getting heavier gave rise to her hopes. Surely a smaller crowd would be more ruly, and only those who truly wished to hear the preacher would come out in the wet. But as they neared the town, the road became increasingly filled with traffic and Mary had the disturbing feeling that they all had the same destination.

The crowd that met them at the appointed field told Mary she was right. Rowland was just helping her from the carriage when a rough-looking man approached with a determined look in his eye. Mary blanched and pulled back into the carriage. Then, angered at her own cowardice, she stepped forward to take her place at Rowland's side. But the man had not come to mill Rowland down, rather to whisper a warning in his ear. He said something Mary couldn't hear and pointed toward the front of the crowd, to a man standing head and shoulders above everyone else. Rowland nodded, thanked the man, and shook hands with him heartily. Then he turned to Mary. "Our friend tells me that the local publican has engaged a prizefighter to disturb the meeting."

"The mountain?" Mary nodded her head at the enormous fellow. "What are you to do? I have heard of bulls being let loose on field preachers, but he looks far more fearsome."

Rowland just smiled and walked toward the man. "Ah, my good Goliath!"

The fighter turned to him with a surly look and flexed his muscles. A murmur went through the nearby observers.

"Excuse me, Sir." Rowland spoke just to his Goliath, but in a voice that others could hear. "I have come a great distance to preach to this congregation, and you can see from their carriages and other conveyances that the people have traveled a long way to hear me. I am therefore anxious to have an orderly service. Now, if anything should occur, you are just the man to put matters straight. Can I rely upon your honor to do so?"

Goliath raised his huge, hairy fist and shook it in the air, causing those around him to take a step backwards. He glared into the crowd, then turned back to Rowland and spoke in a booming voice. "If anybody meddles with you, he will have to take the consequences."

That afternoon Rowland preached on the subject, "Ye must be born again," and there was not a single interruption to the entire service. Before the hour was out, the rain ceased and upwards of a hundred souls sought the salvation Rowland Hill preached to them. "How can we escape if we refuse so great a salvation?" The theme ran over and over in Mary's head. But the question she longed to have answered was, how did one *know?* Perhaps Rowland was right that there was more to salvation than obeying the rules of the church. But if so, how did she find the answer? Certainly, she must seek forgiveness of sins—the Bible and the catechism said so. Certainly, God offered salvation—but if baptism and confirmation and taking communion weren't enough, what else was there?

She thought she might speak to Rowland about it over dinner. But he invited Goliath to dine with them and Rowland encouraged their guest to spend most of the meal talking about his pugilistic tactics and his many victories in the ring.

"I had told Elizabeth she might expect us tonight. Do you object to traveling late?" Rowland asked as he handed Mary into the carriage once again. It was already midafternoon and they had many miles to go.

The fact that the roads were not crowded in this part of the country was a two-edged sword. One had less to worry about when meeting another vehicle on a narrow, curving road; but it could also leave the lonely traveler more at the mercy of those gentlemen of the road, as they were known, who operated on open highways everywhere in England.

But getting back to her comfortable room at Hawkstone was primary in Mary's mind, and she felt perfectly secure with Rowland riding guard.

"No objection at all." Mary leaned back against the squabs, thinking she might sleep for a time.

It was nearly dark when she awoke. "Minson! How long have I slept?" She reached out and took Spit from the maid's lap.

"Indeed, I couldn't say Miss. I've been a-nodding too."

Mary could see from her window that they were traveling

through a sparsely populated, hilly country. A glimmer of water in the distance suggested they might be near the mere, and a growl that came from her stomach told her it was past suppertime.

A light mist was rising, adding its grayness to the dusk, and large, dark boulders seemed to loom up suddenly on the mountainside. Mary shivered and hugged Spit tighter. She looked out the window but couldn't see Rowland. He must be riding ahead or behind the carriage because of the narrowness of the road at this point. Mary shivered again, wishing there were more rugs in the chaise. The cold and damp of the fog seemed to be permeating the carriage.

She looked again for Rowland, peering as far in every direction as she could, but seeing only grayness with dark shapes in it. She wished she hadn't looked. The scene wasn't comforting. She was just considering knocking on the roof of the carriage to signal the coachman to stop, when the carriage lurched so sharply she would have been thrown to the floor, had not Minson held out an arm to catch her.

The coach rolled to a stop amid gruff commands from Coachman John, a creaking of wheels and springs, and the stamping and whinnying of horses. There was a harsh sound Mary could not identify. And then she knew.

"Out of the carriage, me Pretties!" a rude voice ordered.

Spit set up a wild yapping and Minson went into shrieks and sobs of strong hysterics. Mary, who had been inclined to obey the highwaymen at once, was more disconcerted by her maid going into vapors than by the robbers. She turned from her half-opened door to calm Minson.

But all at once the air was filled with the most bloodcurdling shrieks, shouts, and howls she had ever heard. The alarm rang from the hillside and seemed to reverberate from every rock. The clamor was carried and thrown back again by the fog. It was as if the elements themselves had taken up battle and the very stones were crying out. Then, out of the fog rode a fearsome figure with full greatcoat billowing behind him like giant wings.

"Fecks! We've stopped the devil by mistake!" The highwaymen took to their heels. But just before they disappeared into the gloom, Spit leapt from the coach with an angry growl and chased the bandits up the road.

Mary collapsed on her seat, dissolved in helpless laughter.

131

Minson, now limply quiet after her hysteria, sat in the far corner and Rowland climbed aboard the bench facing Mary.

"Rowland!" She gasped for air and wiped at the tears streaming down her face. "Whatever possessed you? It was the finest performance I've ever seen, but you could have been shot. We could have all been shot."

"It didn't seem likely an attempted shot would be very accurate in this gloom—especially if I could make them quake a bit. As I wasn't armed, all I could see to do was to fly at them with all the outrageous voices I could make."

Mary swallowed her chuckles long enough to say, "Quake a bit! They'll never stop shaking. You've affected them permanently with the palsy, I'm sure." She interrupted herself with a giggle. "They'll have to give up highway robbery and look for honest work now."

"Then I have done a good night's work. Perhaps I should take up reforming highwaymen as a calling."

"That would certainly be a unique form of field preaching—and, goodness knows, there are enough of them about."

The thickening fog and their unsettling adventures made the travelers decide to stop at an inn for the night; so it was midmorning the next day before they arrived back at Hawkstone.

Elizabeth came to greet them before they had crossed the entrance foyer. "I am so glad you are returned. A messenger came from The Cedars yesterday. Maria has been taken to bed with child."

"Has the babe come? Do I have a niece or a nephew?" Mary clapped her hands.

"It's likely she has been delivered by this time. I most heartily hope so for her sake. But the event had not occurred when the messenger was dispatched. As our mother is some improved, I should like to leave as soon as possible. I know you've just had a long journey, Mary, but could you be ready to set out again in the morning?"

Mary choked back brief thoughts of the rambles over the Shropshire hills she would like to have taken with Rowland, but smiled at her sister-in-law. "Dear Elizabeth, you must needs take up nursing as a profession. Whatever should we do without your skills? And you too, Jane," she added as the elder sister entered the room. "I am pleased to hear that Mrs. Hill is stronger. And you look much less fatigued than when we arrived."

"I am refreshed," Jane said, "and shall be able to carry on very well now. I do thank you for your help, dear Elizabeth."

Mary left the sisters and went on up to her room to repack her belongings for the return journey.

And Rowland, after calling on his mother as he never failed to do any morning he was at home, then went on to seek his father in his study. He gave him a brief account of his itinerancy, and a rather full account of the highwayman episode, knowing it would put his father in a good humor.

But the Baronet's amusement was short-lived. "I have a matter of an extremely serious nature to speak to you of, Rowland."

The son nodded, giving his father his full attention.

"Somewhat against my inclinations, I have spoken to Bishop Exley of Lichfield. He said there were no favors he would willingly deny our family. But granting ordination to a Methodist was so far beyond his scruples that, should he do such a thing, he would then be obliged to resign his office for conscience' sake.

"He said he was sorry his young friend should so openly countenance dissent from the established church, and he was alarmed lest your eccentric spirit should lead you to a departure from its doctrines as well as its discipline."

Sir Richard paused for the intelligence he had just imparted to make its impression. "I thanked him sincerely for his attention and assured him I bore him no ill will for acting on his conscience. On the contrary, I admire his principles."

Rowland nodded. He would ask no man to act against his own conscience—no matter how mistaken he thought the person.

"And now, Son, I must ask if you mean to continue the path you have chosen?"

"I can do nothing else, Father. It is not my choice, but God's."

The baronet gave a sigh of irritation, but did not argue with what he obviously thought to be gross wrongheadedness. "Very well, I too must act according to my conscience. I have firmly resisted using any force upon you in this matter."

Rowland nodded. "Indeed, Father. You have been most kind and forebearing."

"I believe I have. But now, to continue so would constitute negligence on my part. Were I to continue to support you financially in an activity I believe to be wrong, I should become a party

133

to your malfeasance."

"I would not want you to act against your conscience, Father."

"Nor do I intend to do so. I will not disinherit you as, you will allow, most fathers in my position would do."

Rowland agreed. It was absolutely true—his father had always been most lenient in allowing his children to behave in ways he disagreed with. Few of his generation would have done so. At the first sign of disobedience, most offending offspring would be stricken from the will. Rowland was glad his father didn't intend that, although it would not have altered his determination.

"Nor will I entirely discontinue your allowance." Here was leniency, indeed. Rowland's eyebrows raised. "You are still my son and I will not have a Hill starving. But from today your allowance is reduced to that which will be sufficient only to buy your bread. Beyond that all pecuniary supplies are to be discontinued. My man of business shall be informed forthwith."

"You are very good, Father. I understand fully. As soon as possible, I shall begin a circuit ride and I shall not be ungrateful for any pennies you wish to allow me. My friend Cornelius Winter has offered me the use of his little pony, so there will be no need for me to request borrowing from your stable."

There seemed to be little left to say between the two, so Rowland withdrew to make his plans. As well as drawing a route for his preaching, he planned a call at every cathedral to request the Bishop to sign his orders. Gloucester, Hereford, Worcester were all easily within reach. As to his preaching itinerary—preaching twenty sermons a week would not strain his powers; and besides fields, he would preach in streets and on quays. And he must go to London. He had been invited frequently before to preach in Whitefield's old chapel in Tottenham Court Road and in the Tabernacle. And, of course, the Countess would open her drawing room in Park Lane to him as she did for all preachers she supported. No, there would be no shortage of opportunity to preach the Word.

And so early the next week, after Jane had received word that Mary and Elizabeth were safely arrived in Wells, and Maria had been delivered of a fine son to be christened John Paine Tudway, Rowland prepared to set out on his little gray pony, from whose back his long legs barely cleared the ground.

"Like Don Quixote on Rosinante," Richard said, as he slapped the animal's dappled rump.

"No, Richard. It is not windmills I mean to joust with, but the devil himself." Rowland smiled as he tied his small roll on behind the saddle. "But I think I should prefer to be compared to the apostles who went forth without purse or scrip."

"Rowland—" Richard's concern showed in his face and voice. "Do you need—?"

"No, no. I thank you heartily for the offer, but I have enough for the bare necessities, and the Lord will supply the rest. Besides, when our father reduced my aid, I believe he meant for it to apply to all our connections. I would not want you to distress him further than I have already done. Oh, except for one small matter."

Richard looked at him quizzically.

"When I concluded my sermon to the congregation in the village last night, I announced that next week the message would be preached at the same time by my brother, Richard Hill, Esquire."

And so it was that Rowland left Hawkstone on a warm, late August day, to the accompaniment of groans and laughter.

· 10 ·

"Look, he reached for the rattle!" Mary cried in delight, as four-month-old John Paine held out a chubby hand to the noisy enticement his aunt offered him. "What a prodigy you have produced, Maria!"

Maria gave the seraphic smile she had been wont to do since the arrival of her son. "I can think of no greater delight than to have so fine a baby. I should like to have ten of them."

Mary gasped.

"Well, not all at once, of course," Maria laughed.

As they were talking, Elizabeth entered the nursery. She paused in her errand to chuck her nephew under the chin and receive one of his coveted toothless grins before she turned to Mary. "Your mother said I should find you here. The postman has brought a letter from Jane which I think might be of interest to you."

Maria was fully engaged with cooing at her son in his cradle, so Mary and Elizabeth moved to the window seat at the far end of the room, looking out over the bare branches of trees and bushes in the winter garden below. "She copied out portions from a letter she received from Rowly. Really, it is most vexing!" Elizabeth unfolded the letter she carried and read, " 'On return to Bristol, I paid passage across the Severn for myself and pony, but had not sufficient left in my purse to procure a night's lodging, so was obliged to go on hungry and exhausted.' " She laid the letter in her lap. "I think you know, Mary, that our father reduced his annual allowance in hopes of diverting him from his erratic career and inducing obedience to order and regularity. But it seems the

136

opposition of family, friend, and foe only serve to fire his heroism." She shook her head, then picked up the letter again. " 'I was refused orders by the Bishops of Hereford and Gloucester on grounds of my enthusiasm. The Scripture admonishes us to patience, and I find that virtue to be like a stout Welsh pony—it bears a great deal and trots a great way. But it will tire at the long run. I pray for strength not to tire before my task is completed. I shall next apply to the Bishop of Worcester.' "

Elizabeth stood up, crumpling the letter in agitation. "This situation is intolerably wrongheaded on both sides. His condition in life, his youth, the sprightliness of his imagination, the earnestness of his address—all produce amazing attention and effect in his hearers. He could be one of the great preachers of our day. And yet he is refused ordination over a theological squabble. And he, who could easily mend matters by mending his manners will not give in. I do not know what is to be done."

Mary, who shared Elizabeth's sentiments all around, did not know what was to be done either, but felt something must be. "Is there more in the letter, Elizabeth?"

Elizabeth looked at her hand. "Oh, I had not meant to rumple it." She sat down and smoothed the letter on her skirt. "Jane also quoted from a letter she received from Lady Huntingdon. 'I, who have known your brother from his first setting out, can testify that no man ever engaged with more heartfelt earnestness in bringing captives from the strongholds of Satan into the glorious liberty of the Gospel of our Emmanuel; and it will require all the energies of his zealous and enterprising spirit to erect the standard of the Cross in parts of London where ignorance and depravity prevail to such an awful degree.' I take that to mean that my brother means to preach in such places as Whitefield's Tabernacle and in Tottenham Court Road when he completes his tour of the West Country." She stood up again, shaking her head in exasperation.

"If only he could be prevailed upon to use caution," Mary said quietly.

Both women were silent for a few moments, dwelling on the difficult—seemingly impossible—situation. Then Elizabeth spoke. "But I have not come merely to trouble you with worries over my errant brother. Clement says we shall remove to London immediately after Christmas. Do you mean to go with us?"

Mary jumped to her feet and hugged Elizabeth. "Do I mean to

go with you? It is doubtful anything less than a direct command from Papa could prevent it—and even then I'm not sure." She laughed. "Do you realize, Elizabeth, it has been seven years since last I was in London, and then never out of the sight of Miss Fossbenner?"

"Well, that is one matter we must consider. Miss Fossbenner would hardly answer, but we will need to engage an abigail for you. Minson will be far too busy seeing to my needs in London to attend both of us. Should you prefer to engage one in Wells or wait until we get to London?"

Mary considered for a moment. "I think it would be best to wait. It would be most helpful to me to have an abigail acquainted with London ways."

Elizabeth agreed and they fell to making plans regarding wardrobe needs and packing arrangements for the great remove.

If Mary had found the sights of her entry into Bath surprising, London was completely astounding to her after a seven-year absence. "Oh, but is not the Irish saying true, 'London is now gone out of town!' Clement, were not those open fields producing hay and corn when last I was here?"

Her brother agreed that this section of the metropolis which was now covered with streets, squares, shops, and churches was all newly built. "And I am informed that eleven thousand new houses have been built in one quarter of Westminster in less than ten years."

But the innumerable streets, squares, rows, lanes, alleys, palaces, and public buildings were not so striking as the crowds of people that swarmed the streets. It was enough to make the Bath population seem sparse and Wells entirely desolate. The streets were choked with an infinity of bright equipages, coaches, chariots, chaises, and other carriages, continually rolling and shifting before her eyes until her head felt quite giddy.

The carriage rolled down Marylebone Road and Mary cried, "O Elizabeth, there is St. Marylebone Church. How well I recall your wedding there. It is the most beautiful church!"

Elizabeth smiled. "Yes, indeed. Ten years ago that was."

For a moment Mary thought her sister-in-law's eyes misted. Was she regretting that in that time she had not borne a child—an heir for Clement? It was indeed unfortunate, but John Paine's arrival had secured the Tudway line. And if Maria were to be granted the brood she desired, there would be plenty of Tudways to carry on at The Cedars and in Antigua.

The carriage stopped in front of Number One Devonshire Place, and two footmen and the butler came forward to welcome them. "Miss Child has sent messages around for the past three days, Miss," the Butler said to Mary. "You will find them on the hall table. Each requested a reply, but I answered merely that you were not arrived yet."

"Thank you, Knebworth." Mary hurried up the steps to see what her friend had written that required such an immediate reply.

"O Elizabeth, Mrs. Child is giving a grande ball at Osterley Park to open the season. It is in only three days' time and Sarah is in a pelter that I reply. We will attend, will we not? The invitation is for you and Clement too." She held the card out to Elizabeth. "Well, actually, the invitation is to you and Clement, and I am included. But Sarah's note is to me."

"Pray, my Dear, go calmly. Allow me to remove my traveling clothes before I open my social calendar." Elizabeth laughed. But a short time later a note was dispatched to Osterley Park that Mr. and Mrs. Clement Tudway, MP, and Miss Mary Tudway would be honored to accept Mrs. Child's invitation.

"What shall I wear, Elizabeth? Will my coral silk do? I have no notion of what is worn to a grande ball in London, but the lace is all Mechlin and the silver embroidery on the skirt will be just the thing with the silver shoe buckles Rowland gave me. Perhaps we can fashion roses from silver tissue for my hair. Oh, my hair! I must have an appointment with a London hairdresser." Mary looked in the gilt oval mirror in her room and determined that her west country coiffure would never do for London.

Elizabeth laughed. "We shall see to it all. I shall instruct Knebworth to begin interviewing abigails tomorrow morning. I can see that we shall require one that can serve as dresser also."

Two days later Elizabeth presented Mary with her new maid. Brickett had smooth pale hair, intelligent eyes, and a ready smile. She had lived in London for all of her thirty-five years and had served Lady Towton for twenty years before the lady's death in childbirth. "So I believe you may rely on her advice. I questioned her carefully and she seems to be up to all the London ways." Spit jumped off his cushion and began sniffing at the newcomer. "Oh, and she likes dogs," Elizabeth added.

It transpired that not the least among the excellent Brickett's talents was a gift for hairdressing. On the afternoon of the ball she spent three hours arranging Mary's long brown tresses over masses of black wadding, pommading it, and then powdering the entire confection like the frosting on a cake. "There now, Miss. I'll stake my reputation that you'll be the belle of the ball." Brickett surveyed her work.

"Thank you, you've done very well. And now I trust you to take good care of Spit in my absence."

"To be sure, Miss." Brickett dropped a curtsey.

Hampstead Heath, which lay between London and the palatial home of Robert Child, looked drab and desolate in its winter slumber. As the carriage rolled across the miles, Clement entertained the ladies with intelligence of the sights they were to see. "The place belonged to Sir Thomas Gresham in the 1500s, but the present house is modern. Sir Thomas is said to have feasted Queen Elizabeth there and to have pulled down a wall in the night which she found fault with. The next morning when she saw that it was gone, she was highly pleased with a subject so anxious to please his sovereign."

"Have you been here before, Clement?" Mary asked.

"Yes, to a levee in honor of some foreign dignitary last year. I believe you were indisposed, were you not, Elizabeth?"

"Yes, and I was desolated at missing the grand sights. Osterley is all the talk of the great world."

"And you won't be disappointed, my Dear," Clement assured her. "Every attempt has been made to recreate the classical age. Every decorative motif, statue, or wall painting was chosen for the images it arouses of Greek and Roman architecture or literature."

"But how was that achieved? Surely Mr. Child makes no pretense to classical scholarship?"

"I believe Adam followed Robert Wood's *Ruins of Palmyra* most carefully. And he must have done well because Walpole declared the double-porticoed entrance to be as noble as the entrance gateway to the Acropolis at Athens."

Mary found herself sitting forward in her seat, as if to speed the carriage onward to this amazing sight.

"Osterley was conceived as a pantheon of the arts and sciences and you will find each room decorated in praise of its own god or

goddess—Bacchus for the eating room, Cupid and Venus for the
state bedchamber, and so forth."

Mary tried to picture it all in her mind, but only achieved a
muddle of images in which white marble statues and the paintings
of Reubens floated amid rows of marble columns. But when the
carriage swept through meadows hinting at their lush greenness to
come, across a Roman bridge spanning a lake, and pulled up in
front of the red brick mansion with its neo-classical temple portico,
Mary knew that the sights that were to greet her would hold no
hint of muddle.

A double row of liveried footmen lined the broad entrance steps
up to the portico, flanked by stone-carved statues of eagles with
adders in their beaks—the Child family crest. They made Mary
think briefly of the eagles in the Countess' chapel. Nothing else in
this ostentatious setting, however, served to remind her of an aus-
tere religion, but rather, as Clement foretold, of the feasts and
revels of Olympus.

They had just crossed the courtyard and were about to enter the
Hall when Sarah came skipping across the stone and slate floor to
greet Mary. Sarah's high, powdered hair and lightly applied facepaint were done to perfection, but she wore only a robe thrown on
in haste over her petticoats. "Forgive my dishabille—I am so
pleased you could arrive early. I haven't seen you for such ages and
I have three new London beaux. They shall all be here tonight!
And Roger is arrived with his uncle and most impatient to see you
again—" Sarah interrupted her flow of chatter to remember her
duty as a hostess and turned to Clement and Elizabeth. "Forgive
me, Mr. Tudway, Mrs. Tudway. Welcome to Osterley House. My
mama directed me to bid you welcome and suggest that you might
like to refresh yourselves after your journey. A light collation has
been set out in the eating room for early arrivals. It is such a
nuisance living so great a distance that one must drive upwards of
two hours from London with the whole of that horrible heath
between us. But Papa will not take a house in Grosvenor Square,
no matter how much I beg. Stifford," she turned to the butler
standing by the door, "show Mr. and Mrs. Tudway to the eating
room." She clasped Mary's hand and pulled her forward. "Come,
we can have a gossip while Padlett dresses me. You can have no
notion how elegant my new gown is. I instructed Madame Egaltine
it was to be the talk of the season."

"Wait!" Mary protested, breathless from just listening to her friend. "I want to look at the room."

"Oh, I forgot you haven't been to Osterley before. But let's not waste time in this tomb." She waved her arm at the magnificent hall, its gray walls ornately stuccoed with classical medallions, and statues and urns of flowers decorating the spaces between the narrow benches lining the walls. "I don't care a fig if it is supposed to be a Roman vestibulum like the Emperor Diocletian had in his palace—I think it's cold and drab."

In spite of the fires burning in fireplaces in alcoves at both ends of the hall, Sarah was quite right—the room was cold. "Come, I'll show you my favorite room. The Bishop is staying here—he always does—insists on a bedchamber on the ground floor so he can look out over the park—but I can show you the antechamber. We call it the tapestry room." She turned left out of the entrance hall and led Mary across a passage, turned left again, then stopped.

"Ooh!" Mary gasped, then was able to make no more sound for several moments. At last she ventured, "It's the most gorgeous—most elegant—most ornamented—" Again words failed her. The glowing red-and-gold Gobelin tapestries which covered the walls were woven with garlands and urns of flowers so rich Mary felt she must touch them to assure herself the room was not actually wreathed with living flowers. And in the center of each tapestry were woven medallions of Boucher paintings copied from those commissioned by Madame de Pompadour depicting the Loves of the Gods. Not only the wallhangings, but the overmantle, the fire screen, the carpet, and the upholstery of the gilt furniture were all woven in the same sumptuous pattern of flowers, birds, and love scenes. Mary felt she could stand there for hours, just drinking in the rich beauty.

"Pretty, isn't it?" Sarah asked. "But come, I must dress." She led Mary back across the entrance hall to the great staircase on the opposite side of the house. The staircase was set behind a screen of Corinthian columns with oil lanterns suspended between the tall white pillars, but Mary barely had time to glimpse them or the Grecian stucco work on the Wedgewood green walls as Sarah sped up the stairs, her gown billowing behind her.

"Sarah, is that you, my Love?" Mrs. Child called from her dressing room, as the girls reached the top of the stairs.

"Yes, Mama." Sarah paused in her flight to step into her moth-

142

er's chamber, Mary following close behind. While mother and daughter discussed the details of their toilette—should Mrs. Child wear the pearls and silk roses in her hair or the blue ribbons and feathers?—Mary surveyed the sapphire blue room with its lustring festoon window curtains, a gilt wood cabinet displaying Mrs. Child's remarkable collection of gold filigree and Chinese black lacquer chests. But the centerpiece of the room was the scrollwork chimneypiece and mantel mirror which incorporated in its graceful design a delightful crayon portrait of Sarah which had been made about seven years before when she was ten. The little girl's skin glowed petal-soft and her large brown eyes were lustrous. It was a charming picture; but more than that, Mary felt the prominence given to it in the room spoke clearly of how much the parents adored their only child.

When mother and daughter had satisfactorily settled the matter of Mrs. Child's hair ornaments, Sarah hurried down the hall to her room where Padlett was waiting to help her into the dress that was to make history that season. The gown was of white satin, embroidered with chenille twined with gold threads in the patterns of urns. The flowers filling the urns, however, were not of mere embroidery, but actual artificial flowers fashioned of pink silk and gold tissue. The dress indeed lived up to Sarah's report, but Mary already felt she had seen so much ornamented elegance her mind could take in no more.

By the time Padlett declared Miss Sarah to be "quite finished," Mary could hear the musicians tuning their instruments in the gallery which occupied the entire west front of the house; a steady crunch of carriage wheels on the graveled drive told her the ball was about to begin.

"Shall we go down?" Sarah pulled on long white kid gloves that covered her arms from fingertip to above the elbows and picked up her hand-painted Chinese fan. All the way back down the grand staircase, she talked of her suitors. "Lord Blandford—the son of the Duchess of Marlborough, you know—is frightfully handsome and an excellent sportsman. He's been terribly attentive ever since we returned from Bath. The Marquess of Graham perhaps cuts a better figure—I'm sure he makes a much finer leg in the drawing room—and I do believe he means to offer for me. Of course, Westmoreland is still about. I simply can't make up my mind which one to accept. I don't believe Papa approves of any of them, but I can't fathom why. They are all men of family, wealth, and position.

"Ah, here is Roger come to claim you before the dancing has even begun. Mary, I must warn you what a naughty fellow this is. A few nights ago he came in quite bagged after an evening of good company. It was most fortunate I sent for his man before his uncle caught sight of the matter. But I dealt with him most properly— gave him a sharp rap across the knuckles and upbraided him for being a wicked fellow and a sad wretch. Did I not do right, Mary?"

Mary smiled at Sarah and then at Roger, but did not know what answer to give. She felt there was so much of the polite world she didn't understand, and at times she wasn't sure she wanted to.

Sarah sketched a rapping of Roger's knuckles again with her fan. "La, Sir, and here you are to be an improper fellow again and press your advantage of prior acquaintance upon Mary. I have invited men from all of London to dance with my friend. You must not monopolize her."

Smiling at Sarah's banter, Roger made a leg to the ladies, extending his right foot and bowing deeply to each one of them. "Indeed, I do claim the right of prior acquaintance. Miss Tudway, may I have the honor?" He extended his hand and Mary took it to pass on to the door of the gallery where Stifford stood to announce each guest.

Mary danced the first cotillion with Roger, then sat on one of the gold brocade sofas against the wall near where Bishop Twysden was holding court with a number of dowagers while Roger secured a glass of punch for her.

"But charming—charming. I protest, my dear Mary, make an old man happy and sit with me." The Bishop presented her to his company. "You must know that my nephew has eagerly awaited your arrival, Miss Tudway, as have we all. Do you find Osterley to your liking?"

"I find it breathtaking. The entire mansion looks like—like—" She surveyed the room of gorgeously attired people whirling in the intricate pattern of the dance. "It looks like a cotillion."

"Ah, an apt description, my Child. I take it this is your first visit?"

"Yes, it is. Are you a frequent guest here?"

The Bishop laughed and took a sip of claret from the long-stemmed glass. "You might say frequent, although I believe constant would be more accurate. I find the beauty offered here fills a deep spiritual need, and Mr. Child is a most gracious host." He spoke of his spiritual fulfillment in deep tones of ecclesiastical unction.

The ladies on the Bishop's left required his attention and Mary was happy simply to sit and observe. The Bath assemblies seemed most restrained in comparison to the show of fashion here. And certainly, there was no mingling of the classes here as the spa had allowed. Surely, she thought, this was life at its best. How right she had been to try to persuade Rowland to quit his gloomy pursuits. If only he could be here with her, he could see for himself and understand. Not that there was any need for him to abandon his calling to the church—certainly no member of the company seemed to be enjoying himself more than the Bishop, as he accepted another glass of claret from a passing footman and continued flirting with the lady in a daring décolletage gown. Then Mary was jolted by her own thought. Surely she had been wrong to delineate the Bishop's actions as flirting. No, he was merely entertaining the lady in a lively manner as became those in the great world.

Finally, a somewhat red-faced Roger appeared before her with a glass of negus. "Forgive my long absence, Miss Tudway. Rather than setting up a long banqueting table in the Hall, Mrs. Child seems to have taken the eccentric notion of serving in the drawing room, the eating room, and in the breakfast room. Of course, the punch bowl was in the last room I tried."

Mary laughed, "Like a runner bearing a cup from Mount Olympus, you have returned victorious."

"Does that mean you will honor me with another dance?"

Mary would have preferred to sit and observe, but it did seem that Roger had earned his dance. This was a minuet and Mary delighted in the slow graceful dance as she moved in rhythm to the ornamented music in three-quarter time, forward balancing, bowing, and pointing her toe, which exhibited her silver shoe buckles to perfection. At the conclusion of the number, however, she was firm in insisting on the impropriety of granting Roger another, and so insisted that he take her to Elizabeth, whom they found in the gold damask-draped drawing room with its gilt plasterwork sunburst ceiling, copied from the Temple of the Sun in Palmyra. "Come sit by me, my Love." Elizabeth adjusted her skirt to make room for Mary on the gold brocade sofa. "My Lady Anstine was

145

just explaining to me that the designs on the marquetry tables symbolize sacred and profane love." Elizabeth presented Mary to her acquaintance and the conversation continued.

"On this medallion we see Diana, the chaste huntress, who could give herself only for true love. On the other table is Venus, goddess of a more—er, voluptuous lovelife." Lady Anstine continued her lecture, but a few minutes later Mary was borne away again, this time by a fluttering Sarah. "Mary, you must come with me. I've never been in such a pother. Lord Graham has offered for me—I knew he was about to—but I had no idea it would create such a stir in me."

"Well, what did you answer him?" Mary wanted to shake her friend to get her to talk sense.

"Why, naturally, I told him he must ask my Papa. What other answer could I make? That is what has me so astir. I told him Papa might be found in his library; he doesn't care much for balls, and he always retreats for a cigar by this time of the evening." Sarah grasped Mary's hand and began pulling her down the passage past the great staircase. "Hurry, we may be too late to hear! My fate may be already sealed and I know nothing of it!"

"But, Sarah, have you nothing to say to the matter? Do you love Lord Graham?"

Sarah stopped in her rush to stare at Mary. "Love! What has that to say to it? Mama says that will come much later—if it does at all. One must look to figure and fortune for a proper mate."

The flight continued until the sight of a retreating Lord Graham leaving the library with slumped shoulders told the girls they were too late. Mary was relieved. She had no taste for crouching in passages, listening at keyholes. Sarah flew right on into her papa's room; but Mary, feeling an intruder on a family matter, stayed outside the door. As Sarah had left it wide open, however, there was no question of stooping to a keyhole to hear every word.

"Of course, I sent him packing, Sarah. You don't think I'd consent to your marrying a titled lord, do ye, Miss?"

"But, of course, Father. Then I should become titled too. Wouldn't that be a fine thing? I thought you would be happy. Miss Marford's papa won't let her marry poor Mr. Winston, and they are quite desperately fond of one another. But Mr. Marford says that as she is not obliged to marry for money, she must marry for a title—it seems perfect sense to me."

"Of course, it is perfect sense for her. But think, Daughter. Marford has six sons—each will marry and produce heirs to carry on the Marford name. You, my Pretty, are my only chicken. I will not have the name of Child die out. Do ye think I've built this house and our family fortune and our business at the Marygold for an heir to be named *Graham*?"

"But, Papa, what am I to do?"

"I will not have you becoming attached to a title, Daughter! You will marry a plain mister who will take my name and become my heir. Anyone encumbered with a title will have his own line to worry about. I'll none of it."

Sarah opened her mouth to argue, but Mr. Child raised his hand. "Enough! And I'll just drop a hint to that starched-up Duchess of Marlborough that she might as well call off that puppy of hers. She'll have to rebuild her family fortune with some other heiress."

Mary didn't know Sarah was capable of walking as slowly as she returned to the passage. Each step was negotiated by dragging the toe of her silk embroidered shoe, her chin dropped to her chest.

"Come, come." Mary felt far older than her three years seniority to Sarah. "You can't feel it so deeply. You said you didn't love Graham."

Sarah shrugged. "Graham doesn't matter. But I must marry someone. And I don't know anyone at all suitable who doesn't possess a title." She started back toward the music of the gallery, then stopped. "I can't face our guests and it is so stuffy in here. Mary, let's just slip out to the temple for a moment. I need to collect myself."

From the window of Sarah's room, Mary had glimpsed the Doric garden temple in the west lawn just below the orangerie. And now, lanterns among the trees and bushes made it appear indeed inviting. But, Mary reminded her friend, the chill of the January night air was not at all inviting. "I can't face Padlett—she'll fuss on forever. Mary, you run up and tell her I want both of my fur-lined cloaks. Then we shall be as warm as grigs. I shall just dash on down to the temple very quickly. Meet me there."

"Sarah, you'll be taken with the ague if you get a chill."

Sarah laughed as she scampered across the lawn. "I'm very hearty. But hurry."

Mary did her friend's bidding, and it was several minutes before she descended the staircase wearing one fur cape and carrying another. She dashed across the smooth lawn, hoping the damp grass wouldn't stain her kid shoes or the filagree silver buckles, but slowed her pace as she neared the little building with its four Doric columns across the front. She heard voices coming from inside and thought Sarah must be arguing with herself, when a strong male voice interrupted. Mary was unsure what to do—should she creep away and leave her friend to shiver in the cold, or take the risk of interrupting where she wasn't wanted?

As she paused Sarah decided the matter for her as a trill of laughter rang out. "Oh, la, Westmoreland, I cannot possibly decide such a weighty matter when I am freezing to death. No gentleman would hold a lady at such a disadvantage."

"But, if you would permit me to hold you in my arms—"

Mary stepped into the temple, Sarah's cape out stretched to her. Sarah snuggled in it gratefully. "Ah, Sir, you are outdone. This is much warmer than your arms could be. You may leave us now. I thank you for bearing me company until my companion arrived."

Westmoreland took his congé in good grace, making a leg to each lady before he departed.

"Sarah, you were here *alone* with a man?"

Sarah giggled. "Well, you mustn't sound so fusty. You could hardly expect him to propose in front of the entire company, could you?"

"You mean Westmoreland just made you an offer?"

"Yes, he declared he had been hoping to get me alone all evening and when he saw me leave by the side door, he followed me."

"And you told him to speak to your papa?"

"Indeed not. There's no good to come of that. I told him how the matter stood."

"And so you refused him?"

"Well, not precisely. I explained Papa's eccentricity and Westmoreland begged me to elope with him. Wasn't that romantic of him?"

"Sarah! You didn't agree to such a thing?"

"Certainly not. I simply said I wouldn't elope without my father's permission."

Mary almost choked on a gurgle of surprise and amusement. "What kind of elopement is done with permission?"

"That's what Westmoreland demanded to know too. I told him I didn't know, but I love and respect my father; and as much as I'm willing to forsake all others for Westmoreland, I won't wound or deceive my papa to do it."

When they returned to the gallery and Roger approached Mary to request another dance, she couldn't help noticing a certain unsteadiness as he made his leg. He had apparently been partaking too freely of Mr. Child's claret. She had no desire to dance with a half-flown partner and was relieved to be rescued by Elizabeth. "There you are, my Dear. Clement is anxious we should be off. He has been told that there is a highwayman operating in the vicinity and he doesn't wish to cross the heath in the wee hours of the morning."

Mary snuggled into a corner of the comfortable chaise with rugs tucked securely around her feet and legs to keep out any chill, and let the images of the evening dance through her head—the beauty, the elegance, the exhilaration; the flirting, the drunkenness, the shallowness. The excitement of her friend receiving two offers in one evening, and the depression of knowing Mr. Child would never consent to either man.

As she looked back, she couldn't help asking herself if the evening hadn't been the least bit flat, like a ship with no wind in its sail. Again she thought over the opulence and gaiety and wondered what was missing. And then she knew—Rowland was missing. How delightful it would have been if he had been there with her. His witty comments on the events and his warm eyes and twinkling smile were all it would have taken to make her evening complete.

But that could never be. Rowland would not approve of such an affair, and so she must choose between them.

She was jolted out of her reverie by the coach rolling to a stop. "What is it, Wheeler?" Clement opened the carriage door and called to his driver.

"Tree across the road, Mr. Tudway, Sir."

"Well, clear it quickly! I don't fancy being stopped in the middle of the heath in the dark."

But Wheeler had no more than climbed down off the box than a dark-cloaked figure with a scarf over his face galloped up out of the darkness, a long-barreled pistol pointed at the passengers of the carriage. "Stand and deliver!" he shouted. His voice was muffled by the scarf, but the words and his determination were quite clear enough. Clement stepped out of the coach. "And the ladies!" Elizabeth and Mary emerged also.

This time there was no delivering battle cry from a terrifying rescuer. Elizabeth was obliged to lay her necklace and diamond hair ornament in the bag he held out. Clement followed with his gold ring and the contents of his purse. By the steadiness with which this bandit held his pistol and the evident strength of his spirited horse, Mary thought it just as well there would be no rescue attempt this time. It was exceedingly doubtful that such tactics as Rowland's would have served to scare off this iron-nerved robber who worked the London road. "And now, Miss," he shouted.

"I'm not wearing any jewels," Mary replied, pulling back her cloak to demonstrate the fact. But as she did so, her skirt was also pulled back and the moonlight shone on her silver buckles.

"Those will do well enough." The highwayman pointed his firearm at Mary's feet.

Never until that moment had she realized how much Rowland's gift meant to her. Her fingers trembled as she knelt in the dirt to slip the buckles off her shoes and place them beside Elizabeth's diamonds. Her last afternoon in Bath with Rowland came back to her, the fun of his companionship, the concern he showed for her, his kind friendship, and the joyous surprise of his gift.

She stepped forward, shaking a fist at the highwayman who still kept his gun steadied on her. "How dare you! You should be ashamed! Those were a gift from a very dear friend. They won't mean a thing to you—you'll just melt them down into a little lump of silver and sell it for a few pennies. I would cherish them for the rest of my life. You're just a lazy bully preying on helpless people instead of earning an honest living. But don't worry—you'll get yours. Someday your soul will be required of you. God will—"

Two sharp shots split the air and Mary cried out. Elizabeth screamed. Clement dragged both ladies into the carriage with a shout to Wheeler to drive on. The highwayman gave a triumphant, mocking shout of laughter as he clutched the valuables and spun his horse around to gallop across the heath.

"Mary, Mary, where are you hurt?" Elizabeth clasped her hand. "Mary, can you speak?"

Mary gave a shout of angry frustration. "Of course, I can speak!

He only shot the ground beside me. But to think that I gave in to him like that. I'm so mortified! If only Spit had been with me, he should have shown that ruffian what-for."

In the following days, Mary told the incident over and over again as she and Elizabeth made the endless round of social calls that filled their calendars. And every time she told the story, Mary was aware that she missed the cherished shoe ornaments far less than she missed the one who had given them to her.

· *11* ·

ROWLAND HAD PROGRESSED in his field preaching all the way down the country to the English Channel. In the port town of Exmouth, he rode his trusty little pony, whom he had christened Barnabas, to the dock area, thinking he would preach to the sailors who lounged around the quay, resting up before their next sailing or looking for casual labor. They were a weatherbeaten lot, with eyes that had seen the sights offered by the seven seas and stomachs that had tasted the rum of every port. And they were not inclined to spend their afternoon being preached to by a parson.

Rowland stayed mounted on Barnabas and kept the seawall to his back, which served to protect his posterior from flying missiles and to project his voice forward above the surly catcalls. But at length he could see that nothing was to be gained by shouting them down. He held his hands in the air, a gesture which caused some of the more raucous to lower their pitch enough that he could be heard. "My Lads, I have no right over you. If you do not choose to hear me, I have no authority to force your attention; but I have traveled some miles for the sake of doing or receiving good. I have, therefore, a proposal to make to you. I always did admire British sailors, and I see here some able-bodied seamen. Some of you have no doubt seen a great deal of service, and been in many a storm and some in dangerous shipwrecks."

"Thas right, Matey." "So ah 'ave!" "Damme if I 'aven't!" The response was boisterous, but at least they agreed with him.

"Now, as I am very fond of hearing the adventures of seamen, my proposal is that some of you—as many of you as please—shall

152

stand up and tell us what you have seen and suffered, and what dangers you have escaped; and I will sit and hear you out upon this condition, that you agree to hear me afterward."

A coarse laughter filled the air and bounced against the seawall. "Do you stand up and give a lecture, Skegness."

Another called out, "Thas a ticket, 'arry—do you give 'im a sermon!"

The sailors laughed and Rowland laughed. Sitting patiently on Barnabas, his reins looped at ease, Rowland asked, "Will none of you fine adventurers take my proposal?"

For the first time since his arrival, the quayside was quiet.

Rowland cleared his throat. "Well, I'll tell you then, you think me naught but a havey-cavey field preacher, one like as not to pitch a strange doctrine; but I came not long since from the University of Cambridge. If you had taken my proposal and heard me, I should have told you nothing but what is in the Bible or Prayer Book, even though I don't preach in a cathedral. I will tell you what I intended to say to you, if you had heard me quietly, for I too had a story of seafaring adventure to recount to you."

And he went on to tell, with robust detail, St. Paul's distresses. "Three times he suffered shipwreck. Once he spent a day and a night in the deep before rescue came. If you had chosen to listen to me preach, I should have told you the message this intrepid sailor bore." And to his spellbound crowd Rowland Hill began with a declaration of the grace and compassion of Christ in dying to save all penitent sinners, then led them to the consideration of the thief on the cross, and then to the character and circumstances of the prodigal son and the compassion of his father.

His description of what he *meant* to have said riveted the attention of all, and more and more gathered around to hear. As he spoke, his hearers gradually drew nearer and nearer, hanging upon each other's shoulders as if they were on shipboard. In this position they listened with almost deathlike silence till he finished telling them what he should have said, if they had been willing to hear him.

He then took off his hat, and made them a bow. "My fine men, I thank you for your courteous civility to me in allowing me to tell you what I should have liked to tell you."

An appreciative laugh reverberated against the wall, a far different tone than echoed earlier. "I say we give 'im three cheers!" an

153

old salt near the front of the group yelled.

" 'ip 'urrah!"

" 'ip 'urrah!"

" 'ip 'urrah!"

On the final cheer the men threw their hats in the air, then scattered to retrieve them.

But some remained to talk. "Never 'eard no preachin' like that."

"When will you come again, Sir?" a surprisingly well-spoken midshipman asked.

Before Rowland could answer, a burly sailor stepped forward. "If you will come again, I say no one shall 'urt a 'air on you 'ead, if I am on shore."

"I must ride on to Exeter tonight," Rowland replied. "But should I be able to come this way again, I would consider it an honor to have you serve as bodyguard."

"Oh, going to Exeter, is it? Goin' to take a dish o' tea with 'is lordship the Bishop?"

Rowland laughed at the fellow's witticism and waved farewell; but inside he felt the tension of drawing near to Exeter. The wit had not been far from wrong. The Bishop of Exeter should be the sixth of his rank to receive an application for orders from Rowland Hill, A.M. of Cambridge University. He recalled Berridge's words that when the time was right, ordination would come. Well, he had gone out, following his pillar of cloud and fire, preaching wherever he could find hearers. And that had not been difficult through the late summer and harvest months. He had joined the harvesters in the field, and preached to them at their horkey, attended Harvest Home festivals in village churches and preached in the new-mown fields afterwards. And through Advent and Christmas he preached wherever the village waits sang, and spoke of Christ's coming to earth as a Babe and to the hearts of men as a Saviour. But now the winter months drew on. His reduced allowance was not enough to cover lodging every night, and it was too cold to sleep in the fields where he preached. At one service the Methodist band had proposed to take an offering for the young itinerant. "I hope everyone will give at least a little," the gentleman taking the offering said.

"I hope everyone will give a great deal," Rowland said. They laughed as they turned out their pockets, and he lodged for a week on the generosity of that night.

But as always, the moments of greatest discouragement for Rowland came when his source of greatest human encouragement failed him—when he failed to receive a warm response from those to whom he preached. Opposition and threats served as spurs to him. But small attendance or lack of response at his meetings brought on moments of doubt and discouragement that became harder to shake as the cold weather made attendance and response ever thinner. "Lord, what an unprofitable servant!" he prayed after many a sparse meeting. "Oh, that I might do better for the future."

If only he could receive ordination. Then he could preach in churches, he could return to his family, and he could speak to Mary—the three things he most wanted in this life, apart from the privilege of preaching the Word of God.

As Barnabas plodded the eleven miles to the cathedral city, Rowland's thoughts were all of Mary. He knew there was much lacking in her spiritual commitment. He knew she sensed it vaguely, even if she would not admit it to him or to God. And he knew that God could take care of that lack. To the clop-clop of his pony's feet, he prayed for Mary. "If Thou madest her for me, as I believe Thou didst, make her also the woman for my calling, I pray. Visit her with Thy grace. Enable her to open her heart to Thy calling." His heart contracted as he thought of Mary, because he knew that even if he received ordination, even if she seemed disposed to accept him, he could not take a wife who would oppose God's call for him. That thought followed him like a small black cloud all the way into Exeter.

Exeter Cathedral had been the seat of the Bishop who held jurisdiction over Devon and Cornwall since the year 1050; for a hundred years before that, the site had been home to a monastic church. As he rode through the black-and-white Tudor close, Rowland prayed that in this place of great tradition of service to God and man he might at last come into harbor. He spent his last shillings on food and lodging at the inn and sent the bootboy round to the Bishop's Palace with a note requesting that he might call on Bishop Fullerton to be examined for ordination the following morning.

The reply was affirmative, so the next morning Rowland dressed with meticulous care in a coat newly pressed by the innkeeper's

155

wife and, carrying his Bible, prayer book, and Cambridge papers, walked round to the Palace.

He was shown into the Bishop's study and welcomed with a degree of courtesy he had grown unaccustomed to meeting in the past months. But after the initial pleasantries and Bishop Fullerton's cursory perusal of Rowland's credentials, the interrogation began. "I am pleased to see that you took your university degree with some *eclat*. We need more clergymen with solid scholarship. But what of the report I have heard that in London you preached at the Tabernacle and at Tottenham Court Road Chapel?"

"That is true, Sir. I have occasionally done so. I had the honor to be invited by Mr. George Whitefield to fill both those pulpits while I was a student."

The Bishop shook his head slowly. "Does not the catechism teach us that our duty towards our neighbor is to submit to the king and to all that are put in authority under him—governors, teachers, spiritual pastors, and masters? To order ourselves lowly and reverently to all our betters? Have you not violated this in choosing to preach in places unconsecrated by the Church of England?"

"I hope not, Sir. I love the Church of England. I am unalterably attached to her articles and liturgy."

"And you are not troubled with conscientious scruples in subscribing to them, as are many of Methodist tendencies?"

"None, Sir. I believe no person could ever exceed my admiration of the spirituality and beauty of the Book of Common Prayer." Rowland reverently rested his hand on that book as he spoke.

"And yet, I have heard many reports of your preaching in fields and praying extempore. This is not showing submission to your spiritual masters."

"If it seems so, Sir, it is because I put my duty to God first," Rowland spoke quietly.

"And what is your duty toward God?" the Bishop catechized him.

Rowland answered in the words of the prayer book, in a voice that told they were indeed, the words of his heart also. "My duty toward God is to believe in Him, to hear Him, and to love Him with all my heart, with all my mind, with all my soul, and with all my strength; to worship Him, to give Him thanks, to put my whole trust in Him, to call upon Him, to honor His holy Name and

His Word, and to serve Him truly all the days of my life." As the Bishop was silent, Rowland continued. "I believe I can best fulfill this duty and serve Him most truly by preaching. I long to be ordained that it might be within the church; but if that is not to be, I must do as my conscience tells me, and preach without."

The Bishop continued to sit in silence for long moments, the tips of his fingers pressed tightly together before his face. At last he spoke. "It grieves me to have to refuse so qualified and intent a young man, Mr. Hill. But I detect in you what I can only name as a spirit of rebellion to authority, which I believe to be of grave danger to yourself and to the church; and therefore, I cannot sign your papers."

The bits of snow and frozen rain that flew at him were nothing compared to the icicles the memory of those words stabbed into his heart, as Rowland made the torturously slow two-hundred-mile ride to London. There were places where he might have held field services, villages where he knew farmers likely to loan their barns for his use, but he hadn't the spirit. For once, his passion to preach was silenced. Without the heart to proclaim the Word of God, he had no heart for anything else. It was as if Barnabas carried him along the London road by his own volition. And once there? Rowland had no desire to stay with Elizabeth and Clement, for he knew Mary was with them and he could not face her in his hour of defeat. He considered going to the Countess, but felt he would rather remain free of her authority. Perhaps the rooms maintained for itinerant preachers at the Tabernacle House in Moorfields? Able to think of no better plan, that is where he went when he arrived in London the following week.

The present spacious edifice stood on the ground of the small shed Whitefield had erected thirty years before to assault the "vanity faire," as he called it, of holidayers who assembled in Moorfields for entertainment at booths and sideshows on fete days. There Whitefield recorded, "Three hundred fifty awakened souls were received into the society in one day—numbers that formerly seemed to have been bred for the hangman were plucked as brands from the burning." As Rowland approached the large white building, he could only hope that he would find shelter for his weary soul as well as for his exhausted body.

And comfort was waiting there for him, in the form of a letter from his old friend Berridge. He flung his saddlebags across the single chair his room provided and sat on the hard bed, feeling warmed just by holding the letter and looking at its familiar hand. And the words brought more comfort.

My Dear Rowly,

With desire that this may soon find its way into your reading, I shall address this to you at the Tabernacle, where I am sure you will receive it when your path takes you to London. I have heard of your many hardships. I look upon your present trials as a happy omen of future service. If you continue waiting and praying, a door will open by and by. Be not solicitous about orders. When the time is right, they will drop into your lap. I would observe, concerning your present situation, that it may possibly grow more dark before it clears up. The darkest moment in the whole *nucthemeron* is just before break of day.

Many souls here remember with joy and gratitude the happy times they enjoyed under your ministry. Further, I have received word from my friend in Bristol who reports that "from the sabbath on which I had the pleasure to introduce Hill in the chapel pulpit, has religion been reviving through his instrumentality, and the flame has burned strong ever since. Other instruments may have helped, but it began with him."

It is without doubt, my dear Rowly, that the Lord has blessed the truth you have delivered to hundreds, nay, to thousands. I earnestly entreat you to continue in your work, as multitudes everywhere long for the time when they should hear you again. Many I have visited on their sickbeds who bless God for the time they heard you; and I know of whole families stirred up to seek the Lord by your ministry.

I continue,
Yr friend in the Faith,

J. Berridge

Rowland read the letter three times. Each time the smile on his face grew wider. He would have read it again, but the bells announcing time for service began to peal. Rowland Hill was to preach tonight and he must wash the dust of the road off his hands and face first.

It was the bells of St. Marylebone that Mary heard a few days later, as the Tudway carriage bore Elizabeth and her sister-in-law to Lady Anstine's home in Portman Square. As soon as the callers had been served dishes of bohea in my Lady's best china set, their hostess questioned them excitedly about the young preacher who was causing such a stir. "Lady Huntingdon is demanding all her friends accompany her to hear him. I haven't done so yet, but doubt I can hold out against Her Ladyship any longer. But I simply *must* know, my dear Elizabeth—can he be a relative of yours? I know you are the daughter of Sir Richard Hill and all the world says that the preacher is the son of a Baronet. Can there be more than one Hill so titled?"

Elizabeth shook her carefully coiffured head. "I believe not, Lady Anstine. Rowland Hill is indeed my brother. But that he should be in London and causing a stir with his preaching astounds me. I have heard nothing of it."

My Lady Anstine was clearly pleased that she should serve as informant to one so closely related to a person leading the gossip sheets of London society. "Well, I pride myself on staying abreast of the news." She refilled her callers' delicate handleless tea dishes. "But you must be most anxious to hear him. Shall I send a note to Her Ladyship that you will make up her party tonight? I believe the preaching is to be in Tottenham Court Road Chapel." She crossed to the fireplace and looked through several cards set there. "Ah, yes, here is Her Ladyship's card. Yes, at the Chapel. I believe that is the place Dr. Johnson called 'Mr. Whitefield's soul-trap.' "

As Elizabeth had no other engagements for that night, the matter was settled.

Mary approached the evening with trepidation. She longed, yet feared, to see Rowland. If her heart had been in a turmoil the past weeks with him off in another part of the country, what should it be like now to come suddenly face to face with him after so many months apart? She was at times able to put him out of her mind for quite a whole day at a stretch; but to be with him again, and to hear him preach once more, would put to an end the tenuous peace she had achieved.

But the turmoil began even before she saw Rowland, for the Countess could talk of nothing else. "The popularity of Mr. Hill, and the crowds that follow him wherever he is called to preach,

159

overwhelm me with astonishment and gratitude to the God of all grace, who hath endowed him with such gifts."

Mary looked around at the large Chapel chock-full of those who had come to hear the preacher, and saw that the Countess' words were true. And adding much to her amazement was the fact that the congregation was drawn from all classes of society. The poor who lived in the alleys of Tottenham Court Road sat on the back benches and under the galleries; actors from nearby theaters and music halls, their bright clothing and facepaint proclaiming their profession, filled the galleries; and those of the quality, as Lady Huntingdon's party, occupied the front pews. "I am so pleased you have come to Town," Lady Selina said to Mary in her soft voice. "I shall see that Mama sends you a card for her next drawing room. It is to be a very special one." From the smile she gave Colonel Hastings sitting beside her, Mary had little doubt as to the purpose of that occasion. She assured Selina she would be delighted to receive her mother's invitation.

Mary's attention was drawn again to the Countess' words about Rowland. "He boldly proclaims the doctrines of the Cross, and the Word of the Lord is glorified in the conversion of multitudes. Dear Captain Joss told me above a hundred wakened souls—the fruits of his preaching—have been received into the Tabernacle Society— so eminently does the benediction of our dear and precious Emmanuel rest on the labors of His servant. Excepting my beloved and lamented Mr. Whitefield, I never witnessed any person's preaching wherein there was such display of the divine power and glory as in Mr. Hill's. I believe him to be a second Whitefield."

Mary hardly attended to the singing of the hymn, so anxious was she to hear Rowland. When the music was over, he took his place in the pulpit. The fact that he wore a froth of white lace at his neck, rather than the severe Geneva bands of the clergy, proclaimed him to be yet unordained. Mary was shocked that the fact should strike her so deeply. Wasn't this what she had wanted— that he should be refused on grounds of his enthusiasm, until he came to see he must join the establishment? But now as she saw him standing tall and dignified before her, she was glad he had not denied his belief, and she shared what she knew must be his hurt at being denied orders.

But the lack of a bishop's signature was no detriment to his preaching. "Matches! Matches! Matches!" was the startling cry

160

with which he began his sermon. He held the full attention of everyone in the Chapel as he continued.

"You may wonder at my text. This morning while I was engaged in my study, the devil whispered to me, 'O Rowland, your zeal is indeed noble, and how indefatigably you labor for the salvation of souls.' At that very moment a man passed under my window crying, 'Matches! Matches!' And conscience said to me, 'Rowland you never labored to save souls with half the zeal this man does to sell matches.'"

He then went immediately to the heart of his sermon. "How happy is the man that can assume this character to himself—a sinner saved! Stop and consider—is it thine? Oh, then, what miracles of mercies have been revealed to thy heart! The world by nature knows nothing of our Emmanuel; but the convinced sinner knows that he is lost without Him; he sees that he cannot be more completely fallen, or more certain of destruction than he is in himself. This strikes at the root of all his self-righteous pride, and compels him to cry out as with the prophet of old, 'Woe is me, for I am undone!'"

This strikes at the root of all self-righteous pride. Mary shifted in her seat, hoping that the stab those words brought to her heart was mere coincidence. Pride was not her problem and she was not a sinner. Why should she feel uneasy?

"The sinner now trembles at justice and prays for mercy," Rowland continued. "His hopes from a covenant of works now fall to the ground. Then it is that the Spirit divinely convinces of the work of Jesus; the sinner sees it, and is enabled, as his faith increases, to rest satisfied with the fullness of the work of Christ; he rejoices in the dignity of it, and is happy in its security. This teaches him boldly to renounce all his *homespun righteousness;* he dares not bring it as a condition at first or as a wretched adjunct to complete the whole at last. No. He renounces it *wholesale,* and is enabled to rest only upon Jesus as his everlasting all."

Homespun righteousness? How dare he so characterize her faith built on all the teachings and rituals of the church? Roused temper pushed away Mary's tender feelings. Were it not for the throng around her, she would have told Mr. Rowland Hill just what she thought of *his* homespun religion lacking any stained-glass or incense or embroidered vestments.

But the preacher continued. "So does this new man renounce

the law? Yes. As a covenant of works unto salvation, he renounces it altogether. For he is under the law of Christ, and love to Christ makes him return obedience as his privilege. Besides, Christ has given him an obedient heart. How blessed are they then who believe in Jesus; they have all things, the best of things, and all too for nothing—the free gift of God."

And thus, after an invitation to those who wished to seek Christ to come forward for prayer, the service closed. At least, Mary thought, she had avoided the confusion she feared the preaching might arouse in her. She was more solidly convinced of her position than ever before. And she would so inform Mr. Hill at her earliest opportunity.

That opportunity came sooner than she thought. Rowland, who had seen the Countess' guests from the pulpit, came to them directly after the service. When he had greeted Her Ladyship and his sister, he turned to Mary. "I am happy to see you here tonight, Mary. I trust you enjoyed the service."

"Enjoyed it? Sir, I have never been so insulted—that you should accuse me of being proud and homespun. The Bishops were right to refuse you."

"And because *you* refuse me, Mary, will you also refuse Christ?" His voice was soft and his intense brown eyes glowed with a warmth Mary found disconcerting.

"Certainly not! I don't refuse Christ or His church—it is you who do that."

Rowland moved as if he would take her hand, then stopped abruptly. "No, Mary. I will never do that. If the church refuses me to the end of my days, I will never refuse it. To acknowledge a higher Master is not to refuse His earthly instruments. But we must keep them in perspective. The rubric of the church is not our highest authority."

With a shake of her head Mary shifted the subject, "La, you should hear the Countess sing your praises. Do you turn your back on preaching to the aristocracy? Do you mean to spend the rest of your life in Tottenham Court Road?"

It was as if she asked a question he had longed to answer. "Mary, let me show you where I hope to minister. May I call for you tomorrow morning?"

"Yes, certainly." At that moment Mary felt she would have agreed to anything to get out of those uncomfortable circumstances.

The next morning Mary insisted that Brickett arrange her hair as carefully as for any ball, and she chose her most elegant morning gown and most richly adorned hat. She was determined to show Mr. Rowland Hill what she thought of his Methodistical ways. But the choice of a cloak brought her into conflict with her dresser. "Brickett, I'll have none of that heavy fur-lined cloak. What's the good of wearing my blue silk gown if I'm to cover all its lace and embroidery with black wool and beaver?"

"But, Miss, the wind is exceedingly sharp today, and it looks as if it might rain."

"I shan't get wet in a closed carriage, Brickett. I shall wear my blue velvet shoulder cape."

But when Rowland called for her a few minutes later, it was not in an enclosed chaise as she had imagined, but in an open carriage. He apologized for his inability to provide a more elegant conveyance, but explained he had been traveling on horseback and this vehicle was the only one available from the Tabernacle stables.

Mary felt it a point of pride not to squabble over a mere detail. "The carriage will do quite well. And you can put the calash up if the weather turns nasty."

They drove through the heart of London, passed St. James Park, and crossed the Thames by Westminster Bridge. On the south side of the river the buildings immediately became shabbier, the children playing in the street dirtier, and lanes leading off the main road, muddier. It seemed that a gin shop stood on every corner. "This is where you would choose to minister? Before we crossed the bridge, I had hoped you were taking me to Westminster Abbey." It wasn't just the chill in the air that caused Mary to pull her cape closer around her shoulders.

At the corner of Westminster Bridge Road and Blackfriars Road, Rowland pulled the carriage to a stop. Mary looked at the shabby neighborhood in dismay. "Here?" she asked in a small, choked voice.

"Here. With the Lord's help I would erect a standard for the Gospel in the very middle of the devil's dominion. This is one of the worst spots in London. What fine soil for plowing and sowing!"

Mary could only shake her head in argument.

"The Scripture says, 'Them that are well have no need of a physician, but them that are sick do.' Can you imagine a place

163

more truly answering that purpose?"

Mary again shook her head, her eyes wide with horror at the poverty and depravity around her.

"I would go into the very stronghold of the devil's territory." Rowland pointed to two men in a drunken stupor on a doorstep, a jug of gin between them. "And I would build the chapel in circular form so the devil should not have a corner in it."

For the first time since the service the day before, Mary laughed. "I am satisfied that if he entered, you could chase him out. And what else would you do?"

Three urchins, two boys, and a smaller girl walked by, staring at the carriage which looked elegant to them. Mary opened her purse and tossed them each a ha'penny. They grabbed the coins with whoops of delight and darted off down the alley. "Start a ragged school," Rowland answered her question. "We should get at the children as soon as we can. The devil begins soon enough. If possible, let us steal a march on him."

Again Mary laughed. This was not at all what she had wanted to see, not what she wished for Rowland's future—whether she was to be part of it or not. And yet, when she was with him, heard his excitement, she couldn't help but catch a bit of his vision. "And have you a name for this mighty work you would build?"

"I would call it Surrey Chapel, as belonging to all in the county." Then his voice became quietly serious. "I would pray that the worship of God in Surrey Chapel might prove the beginning of happy days to thousands who are already born of God, and the cause of future joy to tens of thousands who are yet dead in sin."

Mary laughed at his solemnity. "In faith, Rowly, no one could ever accuse you of too small a vision."

They were halfway across the bridge when the rain began. Rowland couldn't stop on the bridge to put up the hood, and they were thoroughly soaked by the time they found a place to pull over in the traffic around Westminster Palace.

The external result of Mary's outing with Rowland was that later that week, when she again made the journey across Hampstead Heath to attend Mrs. Child's dinner party, it was with a sniffle that threatened an unbecoming redness to her nose. But it was the inward result that caused her more concern.

She was more convinced than ever that Rowland's course was wrong, and that if he bullheadedly insisted on following it, she should have none of him. And yet, when she thought of the passion of his words in the pulpit, of the challenge of his plans for the future, of the pleasure she always felt in being with him—but no, that would not do. She must harden her heart to such thoughts.

It was Roger, favorite of the Child family and heir of Bishop Twysden who could offer her the lifestyle she had determined on. And tonight she would put herself out to be all he could wish for in a companion.

· *12* ·

UNDER MRS. CHILD'S CREATIVE GUIDANCE, Osterley House had been transformed for the evening's festivities. A veritable wall of flowers and trees from the orangerie screened the hall from the eyes of arriving guests who were escorted by elegantly clad footmen to the drawing room, and invited to promenade in the long gallery where a harpist was playing for their entertainment.

Mary began her stroll down the length of the gallery on her brother's arm. But they had no more than paused to admire Van Dyke's equestrian portrait of Charles I on the south wall than Roger, in an elegant robin's-egg-blue coat and matching breeches lavishly trimmed with silver frogs and metallic lace, made an excessively fine leg to Mary accompanied by three flourishes of his lace-trimmed handkerchief. "Miss Tudway, may I have the honor of escorting you to the other end of the room to view Rubens' portrait of the Duke of Buckingham? I find it a far more interesting work than this."

Clement placed Mary's hand on Roger's outstretched wrist and bowed them on their way. In keeping with her new determination, Mary smiled at Roger. "I believe we are quite well enough acquainted that you might call me Mary, Sir." She gave a flutter of her painted silk fan like a practiced coquette, but did not feel entirely comfortable in the role.

Mary smiled and nodded to all of Roger's witty comments as they sauntered the length of the room, all the while wondering why she couldn't relax and flirt and laugh without a thought for anything but beaux and pretty dresses, like Sarah who was the

166

center of a group of male admirers on the other side of the room. Why must she be different? Why must snatches of sermons and visions of urchins joyfully clutching her ha'pennies invade her thoughts at a time like this? Why must she think of Rowland Hill when she was trying to think only of Roger Twysden and his elegant manners?

"Ah, Uncle, I have brought Mary to view the same painting I see you admiring." Mary dropped a curtsey to the Bishop. "You will note I am making progress in my siege upon her heart. She has granted me the favor of calling her by her Christian name."

"In faith, it is a pretty girl, Nephew." Bishop Twysden held his hand out for Mary to bow over. "May I hope we might soon address you in nearer terms yet?"

Mary laughed and fluttered her fan, but the unmistakable meaning of those words alarmed her. It was the plan she too had fixed on, but she was not prepared to plunge so far so quickly. Fortunately, she was rescued from further uncomfortable conversation by the butler announcing that dinner was served. Mrs. Child, on the arm of the guest of honor, led the way into the gray and white hall, which tonight not even the meanest could characterize as cold or dull. Long banqueting tables set in a U-shape were so heavily laden with flowers, candelabra, epergnes of fruit and sweetmeats, gold cutlery and crystal, that Mary marveled there was room for the guests to dine. But far out-glittering even the cut crystal and gold and silver plates were the jewels of the guests. Mary was sure she had never seen so fine a display, not even when Miss Fossbenner had taken her to see the crown jewels in the Tower of London years ago. Her hand went unconsciously to the single strand of Elizabeth's pearls she had borrowed for the evening, and she hoped she might not encounter the highwayman of Hampstead Heath. Certainly with such rich enticement as this, however, it was no wonder the villain was tempted to work that lonely road. But then the footmen presented the first course of stuffed partridges, Scotch salmon, rice pilau, and pickled mangoes. Mary enjoyed the foreign delicacies, although the turtle steaks that followed were not half so fine as they had regularly at The Cedars.

Roger, seated to her right, kept up a pleasant flow of social chatter to which she replied evenly until he paused and considered her. "Mary, is something troubling you? You seem distracted. If there is any way I might be of service—?"

167

She gave a bright, if slightly forced, laugh. "La, Sir. I beg your forgiveness if it is making me a poor companion, but I will admit to a bit of disease at the thought of our return journey across the heath. Did you know we were accosted by that villainous highwayman last month?"

Roger blanched in his quick concern for her. "No, Mary. I had not heard. Were you hurt?"

Mary shook her head.

"But, my Dear, it must have been exceedingly alarming for you! Did you lose much to the vile fellow?"

"Clement and Elizabeth were relieved of some gold and jewels. I lost only my silver shoe buckles. They were not of excessive value, but I had a great sentimental attachment to them as they had been the gift of—er, a dear friend."

"Oh, this is infamous that such rapscallions should be allowed to live! May I add my person to your escort tonight? I fancy I'm a fair shot and I'd like a chance at the scoundrel."

"Indeed, you are most kind, Roger. I thank you, but Clement has provided himself and his coachman with extra arms and hired two postillions, so I fancy we'll be quite safe." She paused for a bite of macaroni Parmesan brought in from Italy, then continued with a sigh, "But I fear all the precautions in the world can't restore my buckles."

The footmen brought in the second course and it was now time for the ladies to turn and converse with the partner to the other side. A young captain in His Majesty's Light Dragoons was seated on Mary's left. He was recently returned from service in the American colonies and she encouraged him to talk of his adventures there. "My regiment was quartered in Boston with orders to watch out for smuggling, as the colonials took a very dim view of the import duties passed by Parliament."

"Were you treated badly?"

"Not on the whole. There are many loyal Tories in Boston who entertained us very well. But Sam Adams and his so-called Sons of Liberty were quite another matter. Always stirring up feeling against King George. We had one bit of excitement when a crowd of jeering ruffians began throwing snowballs at a group of our men. When the snowballs turned to stones and the rabble's taunts went beyond endurance, the men used their guns."

Mary's eyes grew wide with alarm. "But, Sir, was anyone hurt?"

The soldier recalled himself. "Forgive me, Miss. I fear I was carried away with my soldier's tales. This is not a fit topic for a lady's ears."

"Fa, Captain, you've begun the story, you must finish it."

The captain answered quietly, "Five were killed. I should not have spoken of it. Politics are not for polite company, but I have been so long away I forgot myself."

But Mr. Child, who had caught the drift of the conversation from the top of the table and was bothered neither by rules of conversing with the proper partner, nor by keeping to proper topics, took up the subject of business which was never far from his mind. "Captain Felsham, are they such rabble, those colonists? What will come of my investment in the East India Company's tea business? It was hoped Lord North's plan to ship tea directly to America, without paying duty at other British ports, would keep the colonists happily buying our cheaper tea, and drinking the company out of financial difficulty. But so far we've not had the returns we hoped for."

Captain Felsham shook his head. "I set sail several months ago, Sir. But I believe the general feeling in the colonies at the time was that the move was an attempt to bribe them into accepting the principle of Parliamentary taxation."

"But why would they refuse to buy cheaper tea?" Mary asked, "Was not the quality as good?"

"The finest Darjeeling and Ceylon, Miss. But they are an independent lot over there. They say they will not pay one penny of tax they have not voted for."

Several of the ladies were showing their displeasure that such unseemly topics should be discussed in their hearing and so the conversation returned to polite topics. Mary found herself unable to finish her servings of veal escalope with lemon and fish baked in pastry. During the last course her tendency to sniffle had been growing more and more severe, and now a headache was beginning at the back of her eyes. She had no intention of missing the final course where her favorite almond sweetmeats were sure to be served, but she felt she must get away for a moment of solitude where she could indulge in a thorough noseblowing.

As Roger had left the table several minutes before, she felt quite free to signal one of the footmen stationed every few feet around the room for the purpose of helping guests with their chairs, should they wish to leave the table during the long evening of dining and drinking. Mary slipped quickly into the south passage which was nearest her end of the table, then stood wondering where she should go. She had first thought of Sarah's bedroom, but that was away on the other side of the house and up the great staircase, a journey she was not anxious to make. Then she thought of the Etruscan dressing room off the state bedchamber which she had glimpsed briefly on Sarah's whirlwind tour of her first visit. The footman who took their wraps told Clement the gentlemen's cloaks and greatcoats were being put there, so it should be unoccupied now.

She slipped quietly down the passage and paused in the doorway to admire the decoration of terra-cotta and black arabesque trellis-work against a pale blue background, which gave the room the effect of an open Roman loggia. Then, a sharp click from a window alcove told her she was not alone in the room. She looked in the direction of the sound, and her startled expression relaxed into a smile. "Roger, what are you doing in here?" But then her eyes grew alarmed again as she saw he held a long-barreled pistol. "Roger—?"

He laid the firearm beside an Etruscan vase on the mantlepiece and came toward her, smiling. "Our conversation about the highwayman concerned me, my dear Mary. As most of the gentlemen carry their firearms inside their cloaks, I thought it would be best to be certain they were all loaded."

"But why didn't you just tell them to check their own?"

"And alarm everyone needlessly? I thought it much better to see to it quietly myself."

By this time Mary was quite desperate to have recourse to her handkerchief, so she merely nodded. "Yes. I shall join you in the hall soon, Roger."

Taking that for his dismissal, Roger left her alone. A few minutes later when she returned to the banquet, the courses had been changed, and indeed, a silver platter arranged with a high pyramid of almond sweetmeats was being handed round. Mary savored a castle-shaped marzipan and turned toward the head of the table where Rapid Westmoreland was entertaining the ladies by engaging their host in a bantering conversation on the topic of love and marriage.

"But, zounds, Child, it ain't always that easy. What if you were in love with a girl and her father denied you permission to marry her? What would you do?"

Always the man of strong action, Child answered readily, "Why, I'd run off with her, to be sure!"

With an amused glitter in his eye, Westmoreland raised his glass to Mr. Child while the ladies applauded his answer and giggled behind their fans.

Shortly after that Mrs. Child withdrew and led the ladies up to her dressing room where they might repair their face paint and coiffures and refresh themselves with tea until the gentlemen should conclude their brandy-drinking and any further political discussion they might want to enter into. Mary, whose headache continued to increase, sat quietly by Elizabeth, in spite of Sarah's attempts to draw her into conversation, and was not displeased when their coach was one of the first to be called for. And she was further relieved when neither Roger nor his uncle appeared to bid her farewell and hand her into the coach. She was quite content just to sink against the cushions and sleep all the way back across Hampstead Heath, without giving a second thought to highway-men or other alarms.

The next afternoon, after three doses of a nasty elixer mixed by Brickett and spending the morning tucked up comfortably by the fire, she felt quite well enough to accompany Elizabeth on a call to Lady Anstine.

Lady Anstine, who had attended a ball at court instead of the Osterley banquet, was all aflutter to hear every detail of the event; but Elizabeth had barely begun to impart her narrative when their hostess interrupted, "Oh, but did you hear of the highwayman last night?"

Elizabeth and Mary both shook their heads. "It's exceedingly shocking. Three coaches of guests from Osterley were relieved of their jewels on their return journey. One carriage was escorted by an intrepid Dragoon Captain. He fired on the thief, but his gun misfired. Lady Houseton called here earlier. She said her husband attempted to fire on the rascal too, but his charges had been drawn."

"But Roger—" Mary paused in confusion.

"Yes, my Dear, what did you say?" Elizabeth encouraged her.

"Oh, what a pity I interrupted him. Roger Twysden said he feared just such a thing might happen and he checked on the gentlemen's firearms. If I hadn't interrupted his work we might have had an end of the highwayman last night."

Elizabeth continued with her description of the evening and then the conversation shifted to the next event on the social calendar—the Countess of Huntingdon's drawing room. "I believe this one is to be a purely social affair. I do hope so," Lady Anstine sighed. "I went quite unaware one time when George Whitefield preached. He was indeed a fine, entertaining preacher, but imagine my surprise when I had intended to spend the afternoon with light gossip and a little music. I'm better acquainted with Her Ladyship's ways now, however," she said with a laugh.

The following week early crocus were in bloom in Hyde Park along Park Lane, fronting the Countess of Huntingdon's London home, where the fashionable carriages arrived for her levee. As soon as Mary was inside, she did not need the direction of the footman to send her up the curving marble staircase, for the brilliant tones of a harpsichord drew her up to the green-and-rose damask drawing room. An elegant lady wearing a lapis-blue gown trimmed in French lace with a small lace cap on her dark curls was entertaining a group gathered near the harpsichord in the north end of the room. Lady Selina, looking radiant in a delicately embroidered rose silk gown, greeted Mary, then nodded toward the musician. "Isn't she marvelous? Have you met her? Catherine Ferrar. Her husband is the tall clergyman standing by the window smiling at her. He's Mama's chaplain at Tunbridge Wells. She's a daughter of old Vincent Peronnet whom they call the Archbishop of Methodism." The harpsichord switched from the Haydn air to a familiar, majestic melody, but Mary couldn't place the tune. " 'All Hail the Power of Jesus' Name,' " Selina said. "Her brother wrote it."

Mary smiled and nodded in recognition and the ladies stepped closer to the group around the musician. At the end of the number the listeners applauded. Mary was so intent on watching the tall clergyman approach Catherine at the harpsichord, and thinking what a striking couple they made, that she failed to notice the gentleman approaching her and Lady Selina, until Rowland made his presence known with a bow. "No ill effects from your wetting, I hope?" he inquired after the initial round of greetings.

His smile never failed to draw one from Mary, no matter how

determined she might be to show displeasure with him.

"I'll admit to nothing more than a mild case of the sniffles. And may that be the worst I ever receive in your company, Sir."

She meant it as a set-down, but his laugh and hearty agreement spoiled her effect.

Then the Countess stood at the front of the room and cleared her throat sharply for attention. "My friends, I thank you for joining me here today on this happy occasion. I and my son, Francis the Earl of Huntingdon, do announce the engagement and forthcoming marriage of my daughter, Lady Selina Hastings, to Colonel George Hastings." A murmur of approval, delighted exclamations, and a scattering of applause met the announcement, as well as a hearty "Hear! Hear!" from some of Colonel Hastings' fellow officers. But the Countess had more serious ideas for this occasion than cheering. As Lady Selina and her Colonel stepped forward, both radiant with smiles, Her Ladyship held up her hands as if pronouncing a blessing and prayed, "God the Father, God the Son, God the Holy Ghost, bless, preserve, and keep you; the Lord mercifully with His favor look upon you, and so fill you with all spiritual benediction and grace, that you may so live together in this life, that in the world to come you may have life everlasting. Amen."

Many of the guests repeated the Amen, then took one of the long-stemmed glasses of punch the footmen were handing around and toasted the happy couple with repeated wishes for prosperity and long life.

Rowland then drew Mary from the center of the activity to introduce her to Catherine and Phillip Ferrar. "Your music is exquisite. I hope you'll play more for us," Mary said.

Catherine responded warmly and soon the women were deep in conversation about Catherine's life in London and Tunbridge Wells and her active brood of six children. "They are a great delight, although I'd rather not rival my mother who had twelve children," and Catherine laughed.

But the men's conversation was somewhat more serious, as Rowland began telling Phillip, who often preached at John Wesley's Foundery for the Methodist Society, of his repeated refusals for ordination, including his last, most cutting blow of being refused for his having preached in the Tabernacle and at Tottenham Court Road Chapel. "I suppose they would not let St. Paul, if he were to come upon earth now, preach in his own cathedral," he concluded to Phillip's laughter.

"But do not cease trying," Phillip said. "I do not say that lightly. Although I had no trouble over ordination, I was removed from my first curacy for my Methodistical ways, and for several years was refused living after living, until I despaired of ever having a place of my own to minister."

"And I despaired of ever having a husband," Catherine joined the conversation. "He would not ask for my hand without a living, and yet with each living that was denied, I seemed to grow fonder of him. It was a most unhappy coil. But I am sure it will all come right for you if you don't give up."

"Perhaps someday there will be a Bishop who believes in a personal God as we do; but until that day we must do the best work we can with what we have," Phillip said.

Rowland shook his head. "I do hope I won't have to wait for a far-off miracle before I can receive orders."

Mary was thoughtful for a moment. "Why have you not applied to the Bishop of Wells?"

"No particular reason. They are all alike. He has simply not crossed my itinerary," Rowland replied.

But that night Mary determined that Bishop Willes of the dioceses of Bath and Wells should be on Rowland Hill's itinerary. Never mind what she thought of Rowland's theological enthusiasm—the situation was intolerable, and she had no patience with what she saw to be a grave injustice. She wrote to her papa before she even allowed Brickett to get her ready for bed that night.

Dearest Papa,

To such a deplorable apostasy is the world come that young men who are steadfastly attached to the church and live exemplary lives can hardly get their testimonials signed for orders.

I doubt not but that you can set this situation to rights, at least in the matter of our brother-in-law, Rowland Hill. You know him to be a young man of zeal, untiring labors, and excellent family. You also know the expansive benevolence of his heart. He is an extraordinary person—far too good to be left standing in a field.

Will not you speak to Bishop Willes on his behalf? Surely the Bishop can be made to see sense in the matter and forgive what others have termed youthful enthusiasms.

We continue well at Devonshire Place. Clement is much taken up with Parliamentary matters and I am

Yr loving and Obedient dau,

Mary Tudway

She went off in search of Clement for a frank for her letter, feeling exceedingly self-satisfied with the piece of work she had done.

It was only when she thought over the fine things she had said about Rowland, and her own determination to refuse him, that her smugness wavered. Catherine Peronnet appeared to be a woman of accomplishment and fashion and she was not unhappy with her Methodistical husband. And Mary knew that by forcing the issue of Rowland's ordination, she was also forcing the issue of her own commitment. He had more than once told her that when he was ordained, he would speak his heart.

The thought of hurting him with her refusal stabbed her heart with a physical pain.

· 13 ·

THE CONFLICT WITHIN MARY lasted several days until she received a note from Sarah begging her to come stay at Osterley. "Mama is to give a musical evening *en masquerade*, so be sure to pack a domino and mask. Please do not delay—I have something most particular to impart to you."

The delight of returning to Osterley, of being with Sarah, and of preparing for a masquerade drove all shadow of the doldrums from Mary's mind. Elizabeth consented to the plan, although she was less than pleased with part of the scheme. "Mary, I must tell you that I am not entirely happy with sending you to a masquerade. I can't think what your mother might say to it. I expect it will be perfectly respectable under Mrs. Child's supervision, but you must know that many seize upon such occasions to behave as they would not, if they were readily recognizable."

"La, Elizabeth, you are talking like Lady Huntingdon. I promise not to flirt with any married men. And Spit shall be with me—he can warn off anyone who attempts to make too free."

Such a shocking thought, delivered even in jest, silenced Elizabeth.

Clement's coach carried Mary, Brickett, and Spit to Osterley early on the morning of the rout, complete with portmanteau bearing a long peach satin domino full enough to cover the widest hoop, and a white satin half-mask on a stick in the shape of a butterfly trimmed with brilliants.

As on her first visit, Sarah flew to meet her friend and dragged Mary directly to her own room, with orders to Stifford to send Miss

176

Tudway's luggage on to the yellow taffeta bedroom. As soon as the door was closed and they could be sure of being out of the hearing of servants, Sarah flung her arms around Mary and cried, "You'll never guess! It's so excessively famous—the most romantic adventure you can imagine!"

Mary looked at her friend in bewilderment.

"I'm to elope!" Sarah cried, then immediately flung her hands over her mouth to muffle her squeals of delight.

Mary could only stare.

"Isn't it all too marvelous! My dear Westmoreland has convinced me it's the only thing for us. And Papa gave his permission—in a manner of speaking."

"But, Sarah," Mary sank into a chair. "The scandal—it's not at all proper!"

Sarah gave a gurgle of laughter. "Mary, if I'd thought you so starchy, I wouldn't have told you. But you know Papa will never give his consent to my marrying a title, and Westmoreland is quite desperately in love with me. I could little hope to do better than an Earl. And Papa *did* say it's what he would do in the same circumstance."

Mary had to agree that she had heard Mr. Child say those very words at the banquet table. "But Sarah, it will never do. You must be married in a church, not in some hole-in-the-corner affair. And think—you will be obliged to travel three nights alone before you can reach Gretna Green. Sarah, your reputation—"

"La, what fustian you do talk, Mary. The Countess of Westmoreland will have no need to fear for her reputation. Besides, we shall be accompanied by Westmoreland's man."

"That will hardly lend you countenance. At least take your maid."

Again Sarah laughed. "Next you'll tell me to take Mama with me. Padlett will be needed here to avert suspicion so we may get a safe start."

Mary could see that Sarah was firm in her plan and nothing she could say would shake her. So she watched as Sarah filled a valise with necessities for the journey, then hid it under her bed until Padlett could carry it down the servants' stairs, as soon as the evening's guests should begin arriving. And then Sarah's concerns took second place in Mary's thoughts when a footman arrived with a message that Roger Twysden desired to speak to her in the drawing room at her convenience.

"Does he *live* here?" Mary asked, as soon as the footman had departed.

"Only during the season. He and his uncle attend all our parties. They're excellent company, and Mama says having a Bishop on one's list is better than having the Prime Minister."

"But is he a real bishop? He never seems to do anything religious. Where is Raphoe? Does he never visit his dioceses?"

Sarah laughed. "Silly, of course he's a real Bishop. He read the service in Bath—that was religious. I think Raphoe is in New Zealand, so of course no one would expect him to *live* there. Now go see Roger before he expires of love for you. It shouldn't surprise me if you received an offer tonight. But don't breathe a word of our plans. You and Padlett are the only ones to know."

Scooping Spit up in her arms, Mary walked to the drawing room. Roger was waiting for her in a green suit and gold brocade waistcoat which matched the wallhangings of the room. He carried a small package. Much to Mary's relief, he did not throw himself upon his knees and beg for her hand and heart, as Sarah's words had made her fear. Instead, he chatted politely about the early spring weather and the delightful program their hostess had planned for the evening.

Mary smiled and chatted and agreed with his comments, but she was finding it harder and harder to be charming each time she was in Roger's company. For all his excellent fashion and ready supply of gossip, she could no longer deny that his shallowness was becoming boring.

She did not find his next topic the least bit boring, however. "And so, my Dear, after you told me the distressing story of losing your cherished shoe buckles to the highwayman, I wasted not a moment, but set my man, and uncle's also, to comb every pawnshop in the alleys of London. Diligence was rewarded—" he held out the package— "and I have the great honor to restore your buckles to you."

Mary was overwhelmed with his thoughtfulness. "Roger—I don't have words to thank you properly."

"Words are not necessary, dear Mary." He moved a step closer to her. "Might I make so bold as to suggest an appropriate action?" He leaned forward as if to kiss her.

As a reflex Mary pulled back. Roger's arms came around her.

178

What could she do? To fight off one who had done her so great a service seemed churlish; to shout for a servant, unthinkable. But she did not want to submit to these improper advances. "Pray, Sir—what if a servant should enter?"

Her protest was muffled by his lips closing over hers. She gave an involuntary cry of protest, but her cry was almost immediately drowned by a much louder cry from Roger, followed by a snarl and bark from Spit.

Roger began hopping around the room on one foot, holding his ankle in his hand. "That beast bit me! If he's put a hole in my stockings, I'll—" Spit held his ground firmly in the middle of the floor and continued yapping shrilly. Roger glared at him. "I'll teach you some manners, you mongrel!" Unconscious of the fact he was holding his injured foot, Roger attempted to kick Spit. The maneuver quite overset him and he fell hard on his backside, making a bull's-eye landing in the center of the sunburst pattern of the carpet.

In spite of her concern for her friend and her pet, Mary couldn't help bursting out in laughter. And Spit added to Roger's discomfort by running up with wagging tail and licking him on the face. "Mary, call this brute off!" Roger scrambled to his feet and began shaking out his ruffled coattails. In an attempt to regain his dignity, he made a stiff bow, "I shall see you at the musicale this evening, Miss Tudway."

Just as the door closed on his departure Mary cried, "Wait, Roger, I haven't thanked you for restoring my buckles!" But he was gone, and Mary was free to hug Spit in her arms and collapse in the nearest armchair to laugh until her sides ached.

The Childs and their houseguests dined en famille in the rose-and-aqua eating room reigned over by pictures of the god Bacchus, then all departed for their rooms to don their disguising dominos and masks. Sarah's flowing hooded cape was of the brightest scarlet, trimmed with gold lace and a gold feathered mask. Mary wondered at her friend's choice of so remarkable a disguise when she hoped to slip off unnoticed. And Westmoreland was no less conspicuous with his great height swathed in lime-green silk.

Upon entering the long gallery, Mary had a brief conversation with Bishop Twysden and admired his royal purple domino and matching silk stockings shot with silver thread which he told her he had ordered woven especially for the occasion. Then she fell

179

under the spell of the Chamber Orchestra de Milano performing at the north end of the room, and all worries over Sarah and Westmoreland's precipitate plans fled from her mind. She found an empty chair next to a lady in an emerald domino who turned out to be Lady Anstine; and so the evening passed with double rapidity as she filed tidbits of court gossip in one ear, and strains of Vivaldi in the other.

During a break in the musical program, Mary accompanied Lord and Lady Anstine to the buffet set in the hall. They had progressed less than halfway down the table lavishly set in three tiers when Lord Anstine's groom came to him. "Beggin' your pardon for the interruption, my Lord, but I thought you should know. After I 'ad everything settled all right and tight in the stables, I thought I oughter make sure of your pistols—things being as they are on the 'eath these days. Beggin' yer pardon for mentionin' the matter, Ladies," he bowed to Lady Anstine and Mary.

"Yes, yes, get on with it." Lord Anstine looked at the delicate slice of roasted peacock cooling on his plate while his man prattled on. "What is it?"

"Well, like I said, I checked your firearm. Your charges 'as been drawn, Sir."

"My gun unloaded?" Lord Anstine frowned. "Impossible. I made certain it was cleaned and reloaded just before we left."

"Bare as a garden in winter, it is now, Sir."

"Well, see to it, Man. You know what to do. Borrow some shot from Mr. Child's head groom if you need to. Gillam, I think his name is."

"Yes, my Lord, I'll see to it. I thought you oughter know." The servant backed his way out of the room, bowing.

"Sorry for the interruption, my Dears." Lord Anstine turned to the ladies and escorted them the remaining length of the table.

When they returned to the gallery, the Italian musicians were playing a highly ornamented suite by their countryman Luigi Boccherini. Mary looked around her, hoping to find Sarah. Ah yes, there by the door was the scarlet-and-gold domino. Perhaps she had had second thoughts of her mad scheme. It was no wonder his friends called the Earl "Rapid" Westmoreland, if he should promote such an idea. Mary twisted the stick in her hand, making her mask wave in greeting to her friend and Sarah signaled back. Relieved of that worry, Mary relaxed in her chair.

After the next number Mary began to feel restless and told Lady Anstine she thought she'd just take a stroll around the room. Lord Anstine and many of the men had by that time withdrawn to the eating room where card tables were set up. Mary could not see Westmoreland's tall form, nor had Roger made himself known to her the entire evening. She supposed he was too chagrined to show his face.

She approached Sarah. "Would you care to get a glass of ratafia with me?"

The gold feathered mask tilted and Mary gasped. It wasn't Sarah's lustrous brown eyes behind the mask, but Padlett's pale blue. Mary grasped the maid's arm and pulled her around the corner into the passage. "Where is your mistress?"

"Gone, Miss." Padlett curtsied.

"With His Lordship?"

The maid nodded.

Mary didn't know what to do. By rights she should inform Mr. and Mrs. Child, even though they were occupied with their guests. But she hated to betray her friend, no matter how improper she believed her behavior to be.

Mary was spared having to make a decision, as at that moment Mrs. Child came into the passage. "Sarah, my Dear—" She paused and frowned. "Stand up straight, Sarah. You know I cannot abide slouching! Now, Sarah, have you seen your papa? I must speak to him—I have been told our guests' firearms have been tampered with." She started to move on, then stopped. "Sarah, why are you so silent?" She pulled away her daughter's mask and gave a small shriek. "Padlett! What are you doing in your mistress' disguise?"

A footman was dispatched to fetch Mr. Child from his library, and in a few moments a sobbing Padlett had confessed all to her master.

"Faith and troth! Is this the way my daughter obeys my orders? We'll make short work of this scheme!" He strode off to the stables to order his horses put to. But as several of his guests were in various stages of departure, the stableyard was choked with horses, carriages and servants and it was some time before the Child carriage could be readied to leave.

Mrs. Child bade farewell to her departing guests, including Lord and Lady Anstine, then turned to Mary. "You must go with us, my

Dear. You have such excellent sense, and perhaps Sarah may be persuaded to listen to you, as she has already demonstrated she won't be guided by her father or me."

Mary did not want to tell Mrs. Child she had already failed in an attempt to influence her headstrong daughter, so she hurried upstairs to change her domino for a traveling cloak. She was back into the passage again when a ball of brown-and-white fur came bounding after her. "All right, Spit, you can go too. It may be a long night and I shall be glad of your company."

Mr. Child and the carriage were waiting just beyond the courtyard. "I sent Gillam ahead. He can make far better time on horseback. He'll know how to delay 'em!"

But it was the Child carriage that met delay. When the coach began to slacken its pace, Mr. Child opened the window and yelled out. "What are you thinking of, Man? Faster! Let's not be stopping here in the middle of the heath. The horses have hardly worked up a good exercise yet."

"Carriage stopped in the middle of the road ahead of us, Sir," the coachman answered.

Mary looked out her window. "Oh, it's Lord Anstine's coach. Do you suppose they've had trouble?" As the Child coach rolled to a stop, Mary opened her door and jumped out to run to her friend.

Then she stood stock still as she saw the reason for the delay. Lord and Lady Anstine were at the mercy of the highwayman of Hampstead Heath. And now his gun was pointed at Mary too. She gave a cry of alarm as the highwayman made a threatening noise; then her cry increased as, with a growl and a sharp bark, Spit sprang from her arms and leapt at the mounted highwayman's leg.

The confusion was all Lord Anstine needed to get off a shot. With the crack of the pistol, the robber gave a shout of pain, spun sideways in the saddle and clutched his shoulder, then galloped off across the heath.

Shaking at the rapidity of alarming events, Mary picked up Spit and allowed a postillion to hand her back into the coach. "O my Dear! You could have been shot!" Mrs. Child grasped her hand. "Whatever next? An elopement and a highwayman in one night! It's too much."

Mary quite agreed, but felt too weak to say anything as the coach rushed on into the dark.

"But what's that?" Mrs. Child leaned forward and looked at

Spit. "Blood on your poor doggie's mouth?"

Mary looked down in alarm, then smiled as she saw that the dark streak running from Spit's mouth was not blood, but a piece of fabric. "Good boy, Spit. You gave that highwayman what-for, didn't you? My valiant spitdog, what an adventurous life you lead!" She tucked the scrap in her reticule.

Streaks of morning light filled the sky by the time they neared Luton, north of London. "We'll change horses at the postinghouse here," Mr. Child said. And I'll inquire for word of our miscreants. Gillam should have passed here hours ago; he'll have left a message."

Ostler and stableboys had fresh horses harnessed to the carriage before Mr. Child returned with his information. "They were here, all right. Gillam's about an hour ahead of us. Good road now, we should catch up. And when we do, I'll disinherit her, that's what I'll do. Cut her off without a penny. If that's what she thinks of my name and my fortune, she shall have neither. Confounded ungrateful—'

"Now, Robert, don't upset yourself. It'll bring on your gout again."

But Mr. Child's prophecy of a speedy catch-up met with frustration a few miles outside Northampton, where the road was obstructed by a detachment of King's Dragoon Guards exercising on the road. No matter how violently Child raged and swore, the King's own would not be hurried or moved in their maneuvers.

"Ecod, I'd tear the fence down and go around them, if the bank weren't so steep," Child blustered.

But there was nothing to do for it but to pull to the side of the road and wait until the company had finished its drill. While they were waiting, one of the officers rode by and Mary was surprised to recognize him. "Captain Felsham!" she called through her open window.

He rode up to the carriage and saluted the ladies without the least sign of surprise at seeing them there.

"Forsooth, Felsham, is it necessary to exercise these fellows on the public highways?" Child bellowed.

"Not *precisely* necessary, Sir. But sometimes it can be—er, expedient."

Mary caught the gleam in her former dinner partner's eyes. "Captain, do you mean to say you've thrown up this roadblock on purpose?"

"Let us just say that Rapid Westmoreland is an old friend of mine." The captain saluted and spun his horse about to return to his men.

"That blackguard! That rapscallion! That—I'll write to His Majesty, that's what I'll do!" It wasn't clear whether Child was raging at Westmoreland or the Captain, but as the road cleared and allowed them to continue at that moment, he subsided. After a bit of silence he added, almost under his breath, "But it was quick-witted of him, what?"

It was nearing noon and Mary had begun to wonder if Mr. Child intended to continue the entire chase to Scotland without stopping for a meal, when he ordered the coachman to stop at the next decent-looking inn. The farther they went, the more shockingly rutted the North Road became and the more slowly they were obliged to travel. "Only consolation is that it'll slow down those young scamps just as much," Child said.

But at the inn they discovered that Westmoreland had not been the only one to be slowed by the condition of the roads. "Gillam! What the—what are you doing here? I sent you out to chase down that good-for-nothing that made off with my daughter, not to loaf around coaching houses!"

"Sorry, Sir. 'unter threw a shoe. I'm just a waitin' for the farrier to finish 'is work."

"Why the devil didn't you change horses, Man? You could be five miles down the road by now."

"Beggin' your pardon, Sir, but 'ave you seen the cattle they 'ave to offer 'ere?"

Mary fell gratefully to the slab of thick bread and cheese the innkeeper's wife served them and slipped bits of her crusts under the table to Spit, who likewise hadn't eaten for hours. She had barely finished chewing when Child bustled them back in the coach again.

"One thing about it, my Sarah won't travel on an empty stomach. I'll wager she's wheedled her beau into feeding her at every inn. Bet old Rapid didn't plan on that." Child sounded smug as he banged on the carriage roof for the driver to carry on. "And spring 'em!" he hollered out the window.

Mary was beginning to wonder how much more of the harsh jolting in the swaying carriage she could endure, when Gillam rode up to Mr. Child's window. "Carriage up a'ead, Sir. Coronets on the door. Can't make 'em out, though."

Child gave a shout of triumph. "Aha! Caught 'em we have. Now we'll see who that lass will obey. Overtake 'em, Gillam!" At the same time he pounded his signal for the driver to lay on his whip.

The top was down on Westmoreland's carriage. Mary could see Sarah's dark curls tossing in the wind under her bonnet as Westmoreland whipped the horses. Then, more alarming, she saw Westmoreland draw a pistol and wave it at Gillam. Surely he wasn't so desperate that he'd shoot Child's groom. Mary leaned toward her open window. She heard the pounding of the horses' hooves, the crack of Westmoreland's whip, and clear above all, she heard Sarah shout gaily, "Shoot, my Lord! Shoot!"

Westmoreland shot.

The next moment one of Mr. Child's favorite hunters lay dead beneath his groom. Mrs. Child took one look at the flow of blood from the animal's chest and fell across Mary in a swoon. With slumped shoulders, Mr. Child got out of his carriage and helped Gillam to his feet while the runaways sped off, Sarah waving in farewell.

The chase was abandoned. By the time they made their way back to Osterley with frequent stops for food and rest, there was no doubt but that Sarah was now the Countess of Westmoreland. "Married in some alehouse in Gretna Green," Mrs. Child wailed. "After all the plans I had for my daughter." She thought that perhaps the Bishop could comfort her, but Stifford informed his mistress that Bishop Twysden had returned to his London house the night of the musicale. Mr. Roger had come for his bags the next day.

Bereft of its company and of the daughter of the house, Osterley seemed barren. Mary suggested that she should return to London also, but Mrs. Child begged her to remain and bear them company. Mary hadn't the heart to argue, and Mr. Child dispatched a groom to London with a note to Elizabeth.

The following week the newlyweds returned, flushed and pleased with themselves and not at all penitent, as Mr. Child wished. "My Dear, why were you so fast, when I had much better parties in view for you?" Mrs. Child asked her daughter.

"Mama, a bird in the hand is worth two in the bush," Sarah replied, pulling a long curl over her shoulder.

"That's as may be, young Lady," her father said with a degree of severity that cut the preening short, "but I'll tell you right now, I've already seen my man of business. My estate is to go to your *second* child. I'll not have Westmoreland's heir getting my property."

Sarah wrapped her arms around her papa's neck. "Now, Daddy, don't be cross. After all, we were only taking your advice. And it has been a fine adventure."

While Mr. Child sputtered and vented his frustration by shaking a fist at his new son-in-law, Mrs. Child drew Sarah and Mary aside to discuss the lavish wedding she was now determined her daughter should have. "It's the only way to put a good face on things and quiet the gossips. I'm determined you shall be married by a Bishop, my Dear." She paused and looked at her daughter. "Shall I have to call you 'Your Ladyship' now that you're a Countess? My, it feels quite grand to have such a title in the family, no matter what your papa says."

"Shall we have Bishop Twysden for the ceremony?" Sarah asked.

"That's a splendid idea! There's nothing like an old family friend at a time like this. We haven't seen him since he removed to London. We'll call on him tomorrow and make all the arrangements, and we must order you a new wardrobe, my Love."

Mary saw the excursion to London as an excellent opportunity to return to Devonshire Place, but accompanied her friends to the Bishop's home in St. James Square first.

As they waited in the anteroom to the Bishop's fine establishment, Mary couldn't help musing on her friend's attitude to marriage—a new wardrobe, a fine adventure, a bird in the hand. Sarah seemed to be happy, but there had to be more to marriage than that.

Her reverie was interrupted as the servant came to lead them to Bishop Twysden. He was in his study, but his desk did not look as if he had been doing any work. He did not rise from his sofa at the ladies' entrance, instead merely offered two fingers on his left hand for them to clasp. "I beg your pardon, but I have suffered a slight accident on my right shoulder." Even under his robes Mary could see the bulky bandage. "Most stupid of me—I was careless cleaning my fowling piece. Now, how may I serve you, Madam?" he asked Mrs. Child.

Without mentioning the awkward fact of the elopement, she merely told him that Sarah and Westmoreland were to be married and they wished him to perform the service. They talked of publishing banns and setting of dates, but Sarah set all such delay on end when she announced, "Fah, what a lot of nonsense. We shall not wait upon all that. We are to be married next week by special license."

Mrs. Child started to argue, then apparently remembered that her daughter was now a Countess and the making of such pronouncements was quite within her rights. "As you wish it, my Dear," she said meekly.

Bishop Twysden waved a scented handkerchief with his left hand, "Ecod, it's an impatient lass. I fear my physician will not hear of my performing any such arduous episcopal duties for many weeks yet."

Sarah rose regally. "Then we shall find another Bishop. I'm sorry we have troubled you, Sir. I wish you a speedy recovery."

Thinking their interview would last longer, Mrs. Child had sent their coachman to Oxford Street on an errand; now they were obliged to wait again in the anteroom for his return. Mrs. Child turned to her daughter to comfort her for this delay in her plans. "Don't give it a thought, Sarah. We shall have the Archbishop of Canterbury. I can't imagine why I didn't think of him in the first place—he's much higher. And I was thinking, instead of some commonplace London church, why not be married at Westmoreland's seat? Apethorpe is such a magnificent establishment."

The wedding talk continued, but Mary sat frozen as events of the past weeks made a pattern in her mind. It was unthinkable, yet the evidence was too strong to be ignored; the pieces fit too tightly. Incredible as it seemed, Bishop Twysden *must* be the highwayman of Hampstead Heath. *He always demands a room on the ground floor*, Sarah had said—but Mary saw now that it wasn't from any consideration of the scenery, but rather so he could have free passage in and out his window. *I wanted to be sure the guns were all loaded*, Roger had said, but Lord Houseton had found his charges drawn when he attempted to shoot at the highwayman. Had Roger in truth been unloading the firearms? She looked at the silver shoe buckles peeping from under her petticoats. *I set my man to search for them*. Roger must have done no such thing; he had merely asked his uncle for them in his cut of the booty. In her mind's eye, she

187

saw the highwayman grab his wounded shoulder and knew it to be precisely the same location as Bishop Twysden's bandages. And yet, it was all circumstantial. Surely she was wrong. A strange coincidence. A Bishop was a holy man of God, set apart for the work of the church. He could not be a highwayman.

However, if it were true, and Roger was his accomplice—when she thought of all his flowery speeches to her, when she considered his audacity in returning her stolen goods as a love token, when she recalled his broad hints that he would ask her to marry him—and all the time he was no better than a common thief!

The very idea! Her temper surged, and the effort of not giving vent to it brought tears to her eyes. She opened her reticule for a handkerchief and drew out the scrap Spit had bitten off the highwayman's stocking. Purple striped with silver thread. *I ordered them woven especially for the evening.* Here was evidence she could not argue with.

She sat staring at the scrap in her hand, too angry and amazed for words. Then Roger entered and made a deep bow. "Ladies, I have just this moment been informed of your honoring us with your presence. If I had known sooner—"

"If you had come in sooner, Sir, you might have prevented my solving the puzzle." Mary held out the purple and silver scrap. "Would you be so good as to inform your uncle of my possession of this bit of evidence and convey my advice that he spend more time reading his prayer book than taking exercise upon the heath."

Before the openmouthed Roger could respond, a footman announced the arrival of Mrs. Child's carriage, and Mary swept from the room without giving Roger another look. But another carriage was in first position before the Bishop's doorstep. Lady Anstine emerged in a spring bonnet lavishly adorned with yellow-and-lavender flowers and feathers. "My Dears, have you heard the news? It's too alarming for words. They are saying that the highwayman is—well, I simply couldn't credit it, so I had to call on dear Bishop Twysden myself to make certain—because, of course, it wouldn't do to spread a rumor that wasn't strictly true."

Mary nodded. "It's quite true, Lady Anstine." And she passed on into the carriage. The polite world would see to Bishop Twysden's punishment. Highwaymen were romantic creatures in books, but one would not tolerate a criminal in one's drawing room. The Bishop's penance would be far harsher than any the law could require.

As the carriage rolled across London to the Tudway home, Mary couldn't help recalling the first time she saw Bishop Twysden in Bath Abbey, with the light from the stained glass window falling across his vestments. And she recalled the words he read, "The Scripture moveth us in sundry places to acknowledge and confess our manifold sins and wickedness; and that we should not dissemble nor cloke them before the face of Almighty God our heavenly Father; but confess them with an humble, lowly, penitent, and obedient heart . . ."

How was it possible for a man who professed belief in such religion—in God and His Word—to live such a life? Could one really become so hardened to all God required that his only thoughts were for riches and position? Would the Bishop and his nephew ever be able to humble themselves to confess their sins before God with lowly, penitent, and obedient hearts?

With a jolt she recalled that for a space of time she had been determined that she would accept Roger. The thought of what she had been spared left her weak—weak and longing for Rowland. For his comfort, for his rocklike values that one could anchor to, for his twinkling brown eyes that could make one relax and forget about such strains as she had undergone the past days.

When they reached Devonshire Place, the sight of the rather shabby Tabernacle carriage outside made her heart leap. Rowland was here. All would be right now.

But when he came down the steps to meet her, his eyes were not twinkling and the drawn lines of his face told her all was not right.

· *14* ·

"LADY SELINA IS ILL. I have come to take you to Park Lane."
Rowland's clipped sentences told Mary more clearly than anything
else how desperate the situation was.

She didn't even go into the house, but bade Sarah and Mrs.
Child good-bye, wishing Sarah happiness with her Westmoreland,
and directed Knebworth to take her bags up and inform Elizabeth
of her whereabouts.

"Has she been ill long?" Events had rushed in upon her so of
late that Mary struggled even to recall what day it was.

"She was stricken with the fever Sunday night. She and Colonel
Hastings attended service at the Tabernacle that morning, and she
looked as happy as at the drawing room."

Mary nodded. She knew how quickly fevers could strike and
carry their victims off—but surely, not Selina. Such a good, kind
creature, her mother's support, Colonel Hastings' whole delight—
and two months before her wedding. Surely that was not to be!

When the carriage arrived at Park Lane, Mary thought how im-
pregnable the great house looked, as if death couldn't possibly
enter. But death had entered the Countess' life many times; it had
borne off the Earl, a daughter Elizabeth, three sons—George, Fer-
nando, and Henry—and now was it to strike again and take her
most beloved child?

They entered the quiet, dim hallway and were shown up the
grand staircase, past the scene of the joyous drawing room where
the happy couple had announced their engagement only short
weeks before, to the small sitting room outside Selina's bedcham-

190

ber. The Countess was there, supported by her old friend Berridge. "How good of you to come, Rowly, Mary. The physician is with her now. We may go in soon."

Rowland went to Hastings, standing in stiff silence in the far corner and grasped his hand. "My dear Friend—"

Hastings continued to hold onto Rowland. "Only a few days ago she said, 'Certainly I am the happiest woman in the world. I have not a wish ungratified—surely this is too much to last.' " There was a crack in his voice, but his countenance betrayed nothing.

Berridge spoke to the room at large, but drew his allusions to comfort the army officer. "How striking it is to see a tender-spirited young woman looking the last great enemy in the face, with as much calm resolution as was ever shown by any military hero in the field—with far more, indeed, for surely more is required where all around tends to soften the mind, than when the drums and trumpets and artillery and the bustle of war have excited all the passions." He then turned to the Countess. "Your daughter has long been Your Ladyship's consolation and earthly support. But the day will, I doubt not, arrive when the mother shall see that her daughter was selected as the honored instrument of obtaining still more excellent blessings. O my dear Friend, the day is coming when it will be delightful to follow out all these now-mysterious lines of Providence from the dark cloud in which they are presently wrapped, into the full brightness of celestial glory."

The Countess, her sharp features tensely drawn after days of watching by her daughter's bedside, nodded at her friend, and then said, "We have every reason to be thankful for the state of our dear one's mind. A holy calm, and humble reliance on her Saviour enables her to enter the dark valley with Christian hope, leaning as it were, on her Redeemer's arm, and supported and cheered by the blessed promises of His gospel. We are in the hands of our Heavenly Father. And I am sure no one has hitherto had more reason than myself to say that goodness and mercy have followed me all my days."

The physician came out and closed the door of the sickroom quietly behind him. Her Ladyship rose and faced him. "Well? Speak plainly, I pray you. This is no time for dissimulation."

"I have done all I can do."

The doctor left them and the small party went quietly into the

191

darkened chamber. The Countess went to her daughter's bed.

"Do you know me?"

Lady Selina's eyes were startlingly dark in her thin face. Only two bright spots of red on her cheeks separated the whiteness of her skin from the pillows. "My dearest Mother," she replied, her voice barely above a whisper.

"Is your heart happy?"

Lady Selina raised her head from the pillow. "I am happy, very happy."

Her mother bent her head, and Selina kissed her. When Selina's head returned to her pillows, she had ceased to breathe.

Berridge made the sign of the cross over the still form and prayed, "Support us all the day long until the shadows lengthen and the evening comes and the busy world is hushed, until the fever of life is over and our work is done. Then in Thy mercy grant us a safe lodging, and a holy rest, and peace at last. Amen."

"And may light perpetual shine upon her soul," the dead girl's mother added.

Mary walked to the window and drew back the curtain a few inches. Outside, the sun was setting. Inside, all was silent with the quiet grief in every heart. Lady Selina had taken her departure with the same simplicity and sweetness that had marked all the actions of her life.

Colonel Hastings knelt for a few moments by her bed; then, visibly shaken by his terrible desolation, he opened the door and went down the hall to his own room.

Mary slipped out to the sitting room and dropped in a chair, with her head in her hands. Very soon the house and all in it would become involved with the bustle that attended hard on the silent detachment of death; but for these few short moments she could grieve for the loss of her friend.

And look to her own soul. The events of the past days had taught her how selfish and shallow she had been. She saw now the false values that must be eliminated for true holiness, which was the only way to happiness. And she realized that could be accomplished only with God's help. Now she knew that it was the shallowness of her own commitment that had made her resent the depth of Rowland's.

But the clarity of her vision, and the realization of how close she had played to the brink of destruction, gripped her with a paralyzing fear. She might have sat there for hours, frozen with her misgivings, had not Rowland come to her.

One look at her face told him of the spiritual struggle he had long known was in her heart. He sat beside her and took her icy hands in his. "Mary, Mary. You are too much looking into yourself. All you find there is misery."

She nodded her bowed head.

"O my Dear, look but to Jesus. There is salvation in abundance. It is a glorious thing to know our sins and to hate them—and ourselves—on account of them. But when this is known, we fly to the Gospel for a remedy. Remember, Mary Tudway is as bad as she can be—she is utterly undone." The bowed head before him sank even lower. "Now where is she to look? Only to Jesus. Her heart can never withstand the power of His grace. Has she millions of sins that threaten her destruction?"

She nodded.

"Then be glad, my Mary. The Lord has received double for them all. In Jesus Mary is complete—the Lord will give her poor trembling heart faith to believe this." He paused to smile. "And then, as she is soon to change one of her names, so she will soon lose another—that ugly *Much-afraid* you will entirely disown."

Mary's head jerked up—"Change my name?"

"There has been no time to tell you, Mary. But at last I am free to speak. You can have no doubt of the love I've carried in my heart for you. But I finally have a right to speak it. Bishop Willes will ordain me. I received a letter yesterday. Oh, but my dear Mary, I gallop ahead. Our friend lies dead in the next room, I came to counsel you for the sake of your soul, and I end speaking of my own happiness. Forgive me. I must return you to your brother's home."

Mary wanted to protest that she was quite prepared to hear what he would say and yet she knew she wasn't. She was fatigued beyond bearing, her heart was full of grief for the loss of Lady Selina, and she had much she must say to God before she could answer Rowland.

He left her in the entry hall at Devonshire Place. "I'll call tomorrow, my dear Mary. Rest you well tonight."

At first, though, she thought she would not sleep at all, as once more grief washed over her. Lady Selina was gone. Mary had known her for only a year, and yet she ached for the young woman whose quiet smile and gentle encouragement had gladdened all who knew her. She, whose quiet, devout life pointed the way to God for many who needed a signpost; she, whose loving heart had found its mate and joyously planned their future—

Lady Selina was gone, and to what purpose? Her smile, her beauty, her love, all were stilled in the grave. What could now give meaning to that life and death?

And with a sudden light in her heart as brilliant as if someone had lit a candle in her dark room, Mary knew that she could give a meaning. Following the values Lady Selina had lived for, walking the path God had shown her, would give meaning not only to Selina's life but also to her own. Lady Selina was gone but Mary Tudway was here, and she would live for those things of lasting value that her friend had chosen.

But even that cheering determination did not immediately bring quietness to Mary. At first her sleep was full of visions as if in a nightmare—she was in a cold, dank church, alone, desolate, and then she walked outside, but the garden was barren, a withered brown without leaf or flower; she was existing in a world without comfort, without solace, without beauty.

And then, Rowland came to her and she was back inside the church, this time surrounded by a mighty congregation, singing praises to God; the scene shifted and she was in a green garden, gathering roses to the accompaniment of birdsong; with Rowland beside her she was rejoicing in a world of beauty, of joy, of love.

It seemed the hours would not move fast enough the next morning until Rowland called. Surely she had not misunderstood him—he did say he would call, did he not?

Rowland's call came at an hour so early that the family was still at breakfast. Clement was the first to greet their visitor. "I understand I am to congratulate you. I have received a letter from our father and he tells me Bishop Willes has consented to your ordination. It should have come long ago."

Rowland thanked him. "It seems the Bishop is not to be put off by my preaching at the Tabernacle. In short, he did not impose any conditions whatever. He said in his letter to me that as the Tabernacle is licensed, he 'thought it not improper and that I might consider my opportunities to preach in irregular places as providential calls from Him, who on earth taught all who were willing to hear, on a mount, in a ship, or by the seaside; and who, at His ascension, commanded His ministers by His apostles to be instant, in season and out of season.' "

He looked at Mary. "But I hear I have more to thank for this happy turn of events than merely the reputation of my preaching."

Mary lowered her head, but her eyes sparkled. "I knew you would not wish to rely on influence, Sir. But may a dutiful daughter not write what is in her heart to her father?"

Rowland laughed. "Perhaps we should consider that you have been an instrument of God's using."

Clement and Elizabeth soon left the room and Mary and Rowland were alone. "Mary—" He paused with uncharacteristic uncertainty. He looked as though he did not know whether to hope or to despair. The imminence of the certainty made his heart pound. "Mary, is all clear in your heart?"

"Oh, yes, Rowland! I see it all so clearly now—the need for a personal commitment rather than just a formal faith. You tried to tell me so many times. How could I have missed it?" She looked up at him with a shy smile. "And how could you have been so patient with me when I seemed so hopeless and added to your troubles with my nagging?" Then suddenly she knew the answer. "O Rowland, it's just like God's grace, isn't it? He waits for us in patient love to accept Him."

"Yes, my Dear. And I am fully persuaded of the truest work of grace upon your soul. Though I know your sincerity sometimes made you doubt, yet your very doubts were to me the strongest evidence of the sincerity of your heart." He came to stand before her. "Thus, Mary, as a man and as a Christian, with your leave, I would be glad to make choice of you as my partner through life."

He held out his hand to her and she readily put both of hers into it, to be covered by his left. "Oh, yes, yes, yes. I have grown up, Rowland, and I thank you for waiting for me. But still I must apologize for my unsteadiness, for making you wait so long."

"No, Mary, not a word of it. Because your heart was harder won, I shall cherish it even more. And never fear, my Dear—you shall be a better minister's wife for all your struggles. Having seen the world, you will understand what I am preaching against. You have had your time of preparation just as I have had mine. And now we can get on with our work."

"Yes, I should like that—working together for something of value."

· *Epilogue* ·

THREE MONTHS LATER, Mary, now Mrs. Rowland Hill, walked through the nave of Wells Cathedral, her footsteps making a faint echo in the stillness, her spirit rejoicing with the lift of the gothic arches. With a smile she took her seat beside the other members of her family who had gathered for this occasion.

And then the silence was filled with chords from the great organ which vibrated the stones beneath their feet. The processional of officiating clergymen and choir, followed by those to be ordained by Bishop Willes, came down the nave and took their places before the high altar. Mary watched through a mist of joy as the Archdeacon approached the Bishop, sitting in his chair. "Reverend Father in God, I present unto you these persons present to be admitted Deacons."

The Bishop turned to the people in the congregation. "Brethren, if there be any of you who knoweth any impediment in any of these persons presented to be Deacons, let him come forth in the name of God."

Mary held her breath. Surely, after all the struggle, there could be no objection now. There wasn't. The service continued with a sung liturgy, the Lord's Prayer, and Holy Communion.

Then the Bishop, still in his chair, administered the oath and Mary heard Rowland's firm, resonant voice above the others. "I, Rowland Hill, do sincerely promise and swear, that I will be faithful and bear true allegiance to His Majesty, King George the Third. So help me, God."

The Bishop asked, "Do you trust that you are inwardly moved by the Holy Ghost to take upon you this office and ministration, to serve God for the promoting of His glory and the edifying of His people?"

And as the ordinands answered, "I trust so," Mary made the same answer in her heart, vowing to support Rowland in his performing of that office.

The Bishop continued, "Do you think that you are truly called, according to the will of our Lord Jesus Christ, and the due Order of this Realm, to the ministry of the Church?"

"I think so," was the reply.

"Do you unfeignedly believe all the canonical Scriptures of the Old and New Testament?"

"I do believe them."

And as Mary continued to answer the examination in her heart with her husband, she felt the next question had special application to her. "Will you apply all your diligence to frame and fashion your own lives, and the lives of your families, according to the Doctrine of Christ, and to make both yourselves and them, as much as in you lieth, wholesome examples of the flock of Christ?"

"I will so do, the Lord being my helper."

And as the service continued, Mary knew that none of those receiving ordination could take deeper joy than Rowland at the Bishop's next words. "Take then authority to execute the office of a Deacon in the Church of God committed unto thee, in the name of the Father, and of the Son, and of the Holy Ghost."

Holding the Bible, he continued, "Take thou authority to read the Gospel in the Church of God and to preach the same."

The Bishop then rose to pray, "Almighty God, who hath given you this will to do all these things, grant also unto you strength and power to perform the same; that He may accomplish His work which He hath begun in you, through Jesus Christ our Lord. Amen."

This was followed by silent prayer. Mary thought her heart would burst with trying to express her praise to God who had brought them to this moment, who had answered all their prayers, and who, she knew, would continue to lead them in His service.

The Bishop then laid hands on each ordinand and Mary felt them as if on her own head when Dr. Willes reached Rowland. "Receive the Holy Ghost for the office and work of a Deacon in the Church of God, in the name of the Father, and of the Son, and of the Holy Ghost."

And then Mary prayed that the closing blessing would be evidenced in their lives. "The peace of God, which passeth all understanding, keep your hearts and minds in the knowledge and love of God, and of his Son Jesus Christ our Lord; and the blessing of God Almighty, the Father, the Son, and the Holy Ghost, be amongst you, and remain with you always. Amen."

THE END

· *Historical Note* ·

IN TELLING THIS STORY, I have blended four true accounts from the late 1700s. As fanciful as it may seem, Bishop Twysden's story is true, as, unfortunately, is the death of Lady Selina.

The Earl of Westmoreland became Viceroy of Ireland, and Lady Westmoreland, the Vicerene. True to the terms of Robert Child's will, Osterley passed to Sarah Sophia Fane, Lady Westmoreland's second child who married George Villiers. He took the name Child-Villiers and became the fifth Earl of Jersey. Readers of Regency romances will recognize her as "Queen Sarah," the Countess of Jersey, one of the famous committee who ruled on rights of admission to Almack's.

Rowland Hill and Mary Tudway were married in June of 1773 at the Church of St. Marylebone in London. He was ordained Deacon that same month by Dr. Willes, Bishop of Bath and Wells. At the insistence of the Archbishop of York, however, he was never granted Priest's orders and so was, he said, "required to go through life with only one shoe on." His parish was on the green banks of the Severn at Wotton-under-edge in Gloucestershire, and he built Surrey Chapel, as he foresaw—"round so the devil should not have a corner in it." Attached to the chapel were thirteen Sunday Schools with over three thousand children on their rolls. Later in life he described himself as "rector of Surrey Chapel, vicar of Wotton-under-edge, and curate of all the fields, commons, and pastures throughout England and Wales."

I wish to express my special appreciation to Mr. David Tudway Quilter who sent me his excellent book on his family's history; to the librarians at the Huntingdon Centre at The Countess of Huntingdon's Chapel, especially Andrew Ballinger and Ayeli Barett; and at Wesley's Chapel, Mr. Cyril Skinner, Managing Curator, and Rev. Douglas A. Wollen, Historian.

Donna Fletcher Crow
Boise, Idaho
1988

WORD LIST

Adam—Robert Adam, 1728-1792, leading English architect

Bagged—drunk

Beard the master in his den—to confront with boldness, to defy.
As in: "And dar'st thou then
To beard the lion in his den,
The Douglas in his hall?
An hop'st thou thence unscathed to go?"
Sir Walter Scott, *Marmion*

Beau Nash—1674-1761, Master of Ceremonies of Bath, called its "uncrowned king"

Bohea—black tea

Bonze—Buddhist monk

Calash—folding top of a small, light-wheeled carriage; a style of woman's cap resembling the carriage top

Congé—dismissal

Conventicling—preaching in an unconsecreated place

Couple—a musical episode, as a rondo

Domino—long, loose, hooded cloak worn as masquerade costume

Don—a head, tutor, or fellow in a college at Oxford or Cambridge

Exhibition—a grant drawn from the funds of a school to help maintain a student

François Boucher—French painter, 1703—1770

Frank—free postage, granted by Member of Parliament, or Peer of the Realm

Grig—lighthearted child

Gownsman—member of the university

Havey-cavey—unsteady, helter-skelter

Honored in the breach—alludes to
"But to my mind,—though I am native here,
And to the manner born,—it is a custom
More honour'd in the breach than the observance."
William Shakespeare, *Hamlet*

Horkey—harvest dinner

Macaroni—member of a class of young Englishmen that affected foreign ways; dandy

Marcher—an inhabitant of the border between Wales and England

Marchpane—marzipan

199

Mechlin—delicate bobbin lace made in Mechlin, Belgium

Mere—lake

Nicodemus chamber—"closet" in the Countess' chapel for bishops who did not wish to be seen at the service

Nucthemeron—a calendar of hours

Opprobrium—something that brings disgrace

Parterre—ornamental garden

Peg tower—a statement used as a support or reason

Postillion—one who rides as a guide to a coach

Publican—innkeeper, keeper of a public house

Squab—cushion

The Tabernacle—a chapel established in 1741 for the preaching of George Whitefield and others in Moorfields, London, near Wesley's Foundery

Tenterfield—field used for drying or stretching cloth

To make a leg—to bow with the leg extended in front

Tottenham Court Chapel—erected by George Whitefield in the west end of London in 1756

Turnkey—one who has charge of a prison's keys

Whipt syllabub—a frothy, sweet dessert made of cream and liquor

MAJOR REFERENCES

V.J. Charlesworth, *Rowland Hill, His Life, Anecdotes, & Pulpit Sayings*, London: Hodder & Stroughton, 1877.

Willard Connely, *Beau Nash, Monarch of Bath and Tunbridge Wells*, London: Werner Laurie, 1955.

Earl of Jersey, *Osterley Park Isleworth*, A guide for Visitors, London: G. White, n.d.

John Hardy, Maurice Tomlin, *Osterley Park House*, London: The Victoria and Albert Museum, 1985.

Rowland Hill, "Glorious Displays of Gospel Grace," in *Missionary Sermons*, London: T. Chapman, 1796.

Rowland Hill, *The Sale of Curates by Public Auction*, London: M. Jones, 1803.

Rowland Hill, Recommendatory Preface to *Refuge for the Prisoner of Hope*, London: M. Lewiss, 1772.

Rowland Hill, Unpublished letters to his sister, by permission of the Masters and Fellows of St. John's College.

William Jones, M.A., *Memoirs of the Life, Ministry, and Writings of the Rev. Rowland Hill, M.A. Late Minister of Surrey Chapel*, London: John Bennett, 1834.

Gilbert W. Kirby, *The Elect Lady*, Trustees of the Countess of Huntingdon's Connexion, 1972.

Helen C. Knight, *Lady Huntington* (sic.) *And Her Friends; the Revival of the Work of God*, New York: American Tract Society, 1853.

Lewis Melville, *Bath Under Beau Nash*, London: Eveleigh Nash, 1907.

A Member of the Houses of Shirley and Hastings, *The Life and Times of Selina, Countess of Huntingdon*, vols. I & II, London, William Edward Painter, 1833.

Edward Miller, *Portrait of a College: A History of the College of Saint John the Evangelist in Cambridge*, Cambridge Universtiy Press, 1961.

R.S. Neale, *Bath, A Social History 1680–1850* or *A Valley of Pleasure, Yet a Sink of Iniquity*, London: Routledge & Kegan Paul, 1981.

Rev. John Penrose, Bridgette Mitchell, and Hubert Penrose, eds. *Letters from Bath 1766–1767*, Gloucester: Alan Sutton, 1983.

David Tudway Quilter, "The Cedars and The Tudways," in *Wells Cathedral School*, Wells: Clare Son and Co., Ltd.

T. Rodenhurst, *A Description of Hawkstone, the Seat of Sir John Hill, Bart*, London: John Stockdale, 1811.

Benjamin Senior, *A Hundred Years at Surrey Chapel*, London: Passmore & Alabaster, 1892.

Rev. Edwin Sidney, A.M. *The Life of the Rev. Rowland Hill, A.M.*, London: Baldwin & Cradock, 1834.

R.A.L. Smith, *Bath*, London: B.T. Batsford, Ltd., 1944.

Sarah Tytler, *The Countess of Huntingdon and her Circle*, London: Sir Isaac Pitman & Sons, Ltd., 1907.

Peter Ward-Jackson, *Guide to Osterley Park*, London: Her Majesty's Stationery Office, 1954.

Memoirs of the Rev. Rowland Hill, A.M., London: Thomas Ward & Co., 1835.

Book of Common Prayer, Oxford: T. Wright and W. Gill, 1773.

TIME LINE FOR THE
CAMBRIDGE COLLECTION

UNITED STATES

ENGLAND

George Whitefield begins preaching	1738	John Wesley's Aldersgate Experience
	1740	
French and Indian War	1756	
	1760	George III crowned
	1765	Lady Huntingdon opens chapel in Bath
	1766	Stamp Act passed
Boston Tea Party	1773	Rowland Hill ordained
The Revolutionary War	1776	The American War
	1787	Wilberforce begins antislavery campaign
Constitution ratified	1788	
George Washington elected president	1789	
	1799	Church Missionary Society founded
	1805	Lord Nelson wins Battle of Trafalgar
	1807	Parliament bans slave trade
War of 1812	1812	Charles Simeon begins Conversation Parties
	1815	Waterloo
Missouri Compromise	1820	George IV crowned
John Quincy Adams elected president	1825	
	1830	William IV crowned
Temperance Union founded	1833	William Wilberforce dies
Texas Independence	1836	Charles Simeon dies
	1837	Queen Victoria crowned
Susan B. Anthony Campaigns	1848	
California Gold Rush	1849	
	1851	Crystal Palace opens
Uncle Tom's Cabin published	1852	
	1854	Florence Nightingale goes to Crimean War
	1858	George MacDonald publishes *Phantastes*
Abraham Lincoln elected president	1860	
Emancipation Proclamation	1863	
	1865	Hudson Taylor founds China Inland Mission
Transcontinental Railroad completed	1869	
	1877	D.L. Moody and Ira Sankey London Revivals
Thomas Edison invents lightbulb	1879	
	1885	Cambridge Seven joins China Inland Mission

FICTION FROM VICTOR BOOKS

George MacDonald

A Quiet Neighborhood
The Seaboard Parish
The Vicar's Daughter
The Shopkeeper's Daughter
The Last Castle
The Prodigal Apprentice
On Tangled Paths
Heather and Snow

Cliff Schimmels

The Wheatheart Chronicles
Winter Hunger
Rivals of Spring
Summer Winds
Rites of Autumn

Donna Fletcher Crow

The Cambridge Collection
Brandley's Search
To Be Worthy
A Gentle Calling
Something of Value

Robert Wise

The Pastors' Barracks
The Scrolls of Edessa